RICHIE MCCAW

A Tribute to a Modern-day Rugby Great

RICHIE McCAW

A Tribute to a Modern-day Rugby Great

John Matheson/Celebrity Portraits

Richie McCaw and Keven Mealamu prepare for battle at Newlands
in Cape Town before taking it to the Springboks in the 2008.

At one time Crusaders' rugby bosses wondered how they would replace the great Todd Blackadder as leaders of the red-and-blacks. Reuben Thorne was a solid replacement but Richie McCaw has taking the role to even higher levels.

CONTENTS

Richie McCaw's pedigree as a leader is unquestionable,
his grandfather being New Zealand war hero Jim McCaw,
who took on Adolf Hilter's best as he helped defend
Great Britain in the Second World War.

THE NEXT BIG THING

JIM McCaw fought in the skies over France during the Second World War, intercepting Adolf Hitler's V1 flying bombs on their deadly path to London. According to the Royal New Zealand Air Force pilots who flew under his command from their base in Kent, McCaw shot down 20 dreaded 'doodlebugs' before they could cross the Channel. The war over, McCaw went home to New Zealand, raised a family and ran a flying school. His grandson, Richie, is captain of the All Blacks.

With that pedigree there should be no surprise that McCaw is one of only two All Blacks captains to have emerged from the helm of a World Cup disaster with his reputation very much intact. In a country like New Zealand, that is akin to a deserting soldier avoiding the firing squad.

The list of captains who have been unable to achieve such status includes men who, had it not been for their World Cup failures, could expect to be enshrined as 'greats'. Instead, regardless of the heights they reached outside of the tournaments, they are forever linked to their failures.

Gary Whetton was a part of the team that won the inaugural World Cup in 1987 . . . but is remembered most for his team's failure in a semifinal against Australia four years later. Taine Randell was one of the most gifted loose forwards to wear the black jersey in the professional era — equally at home at No. 8 or on the blindside. But despite playing for the All Blacks on 61 occasions, the one game that lingers in the memory is the capitulation against France in 1999, when his team — after leading by 14 points in the second half — lost 31–43. Four years later, it was Reuben Thorne's turn. Stoic and proud, everything he did was for the team. His was a style of 'Do not what I say; do as I do.' He enjoyed extraordinary success as a captain of the Crusaders. But as an All Blacks skipper — despite leading the team to a Tri-Nations sweep in 2003 (including wrestling the Bledisloe Cup off Australia for the first time since it was lost in 1998) — he is remembered, harshly as it is, as a loser. That's what happens when your team loses a semifinal to Australia.

One of the two captains to lose in a World Cup

with his reputation fully intact was Sean Fitzpatrick. Indeed, if anything, his reputation grew stronger after his side lost the 1995 final against hosts South Africa in controversial circumstances. He dusted himself off, and a year later was back in the Republic leading New Zealand to its first series win on Springbok soil.

The other exception to the rule, of course, is McCaw. And that's remarkable when you consider his All Blacks team in 2007 was bundled out of the World Cup in the quarterfinal phase — New Zealand's worst showing at rugby's showpiece event. That he has retained not only the job as skipper, but has taken his performances, leadership and standing with the rugby nation to new levels, says much about the make-up of the man. He is, in every sense, a throwback to a by-gone era when All Blacks were cast in the role of humble heroes; men whose characteristics were

ABOVE: Sean Fitzpatrick is an unusual phenomenon in New Zealand rugby — he captained an unsuccessful All Blacks World Cup side but came through the experience with his reputation fully intact.

RIGHT: Richie McCaw in typical pose — on the charge against the All Blacks' greatest foes, the Springboks.

blended from an understated killer instinct and an ability to deal with pressure while those around them were beginning to second-guess themselves.

They're the same qualities that a certain Flight Lieutenant Jim McCaw possessed all those years ago. Thank goodness that today's battlefields for young men from New Zealand are the rugby stadiums of the world.

TODD Blackadder was never one to heap praise on individuals. As the long-time Canterbury and Crusaders captain, he was all about concepts like 'the team' and 'the jersey'. When praise came his way, he would almost always deflect it with the time-honoured 'The team did everything . . . I just ended up in the right place' token quote for the media throng. So it was quite something for Blackadder to break with that particular tradition. The occasion that saw him let his guard down happened to be the day Richie McCaw played his first game against Otago.

McCaw had been slowly working his way through the red-and-black ranks. It was 2001 and he had just bounced back from an eye injury that had stopped him in his tracks the previous season. McCaw was playing for Canterbury Colts against Southland when he suffered a crack in his eye orbital, 'which jammed up a bit of muscle that moves the eye'. He had to have an operation to free it up, but was unable to move his left eye for four days until he had surgery. His sight was never at risk, but it was still a worrying time for the then New Zealand age-group representative. It would be two months after the operation before he could rid himself of double vision.

He'd recovered sufficiently to play for the Crusaders Colts in 2001, however, and had even made his Super 12 debut as a replacement for injured flanker Reuben Thorne. He'd also captained the New Zealand Colts team to victory in the Southern Hemisphere Under-21 tournament final after his Canterbury teammate

Richie McCaw has always had great support from his family: parents, Don and Margaret, and sister, Joanna.

Aaron Mauger, the original skipper, was ruled out by injury. A knee injury and pulled a muscle in his hip then conspired to keep McCaw out of Canterbury's NPC side for the first two games against Northland and Southland. But in the third game of the campaign, he won his first run-on roll — he'd appeared off the bench for his province against North Harbour in 2000 — for Steve Hansen's team against Bay of Plenty. He did enough to hold his position for the next game against Harbour, and by the time of the Otago game people were beginning to take notice of the tearaway flanker.

The game at Carisbrook — a match that would become his break-out performance — was one the 20-year-old McCaw had been focused on since the fixtures for the season had been published months before. Hailing from the Hakataramea Valley in North Otago, he'd gone to school in Dunedin at Otago Boys' High School. After spending two years in the First XV as a No. 8 and openside flanker, he left Otago rugby's catchment area when he struck out for Lincoln University, where he was doing an agricultural science degree. As a schoolboy, though, he was a regular on the terraces when Otago played at home. 'It's going to be a big thrill running out there at Carisbrook,' he said before the game. As a student spectator, McCaw's main idol had been Otago's All Black flanker Josh Kronfeld. 'He's the best [openside flanker] we've had for a long time.'

Even in 2001 McCaw was in the Kronfeld–George Smith style, specializing in getting quickly to the breakdowns and scrabbling for the ball. His defence and support play had earmarked him as a player for the future. 'I believe that's what a seven should be doing, winning the ball and leaving the ball playing to the other two [loose forwards]. If you can secure a couple of turnovers, that can change the nature of the game.'

Changing the nature of the game is just what McCaw did that September night. Remarkably, he scored three tries in 25 minutes as he set the red-and-blacks on their way to an extraordinary 62–19 win against Laurie Mains's Otago — the team Canterbury would eventually met in the NPC final. McCaw's first touchdown, after nine minutes, was a fitting reward. He created a turnover by ripping the ball away from All Black Pita Alatini in a ruck in Canterbury's half, and he was on hand to score after a brilliant break by fullback Leon MacDonald with assistance from Caleb Ralph. Ralph set up McCaw's second soon after with a slashing break from a set move, and the youngster snapped up his third try after hooker Matt Sexton was tackled near the Otago posts and Andrew Mehrtens spread it quickly. He may well have had four, but he was subbed off in the final quarter, and his replacement Sam Broomhall scored with his first touch of the ball.

But it wasn't only the hat-trick that set McCaw apart. His support play was superb, and his tackling stopped Otago opponents in their tracks. In short, he showed that he was already the Real McCaw. The local paper called him *The Next Big Thing*. And Blackadder — the ultimate 'there's no *i* in team' man — couldn't help himself either. 'He's a great talent. If you look around New Zealand there are some talented number sevens and he's certainly one of those,' Blackadder said. 'If you're wanting to counter the likes of George Smith and are looking for the next Josh Kronfeld, then look no further than Richie McCaw.'

Hansen, too, was singing the prodigy's praise. 'He did what we always knew he could do,' Hansen told the press. 'That's why we've always looked after him. He's still pretty young, and we just need to make sure he's looked after because we need him to play for a long time. We knew Richie had all the attributes a good openside flanker needs. He is very brave on the ball, he is a strong tackler and he is intelligent. He has a remarkable sense of where to be out there. A remarkable sense of timing.'

McCaw, who clearly had huge natural gifts and intelligence, had the bonus of playing alongside seasoned, but still vigorous, players like No. 8 Scott Robertson and blindside flanker Reuben Thorne. He

'By the end of the season he'll be the best
number seven in the country.
There's really nothing he can't do.'

was learning his trade in the best breeding ground in New Zealand rugby and, as the juggernaut that was Hansen's team continued its dominance in 2001, McCaw was stealing headlines at every turn. That man Blackadder, again, waxing lyrical: 'By the end of the season he'll be the best number seven in the country. There's really nothing he can't do. He's big, but he gets the ball on the ground, he can run, and he's a great tackler. Barring injury, who knows how good he'll turn out to be.'

McCaw was instrumental in shutting down Auckland's mercurial No. 10 Carlos Spencer when the boys from the Big Smoke challenged for the Ranfurly Shield at Lancaster Park, a game won by the home side 38–10. A week later, when Waikato challenged, he outplayed Marty Holah, who'd had racked up seven tests for the All Blacks earlier in the year as he shared the No. 7 duties with Taine Randell while the New Zealand selectors searched for a replacement for the now-retired Josh Kronfeld.

When Auckland returned for their semifinal, McCaw again was dominant, and was one of six try scorers for Canterbury in a 53–25 rout. Seven days later, in his first season in the NPC, McCaw was starting in his first final. Otago were bolstered by returning All Blacks Anton Oliver, Byron Kelleher and Randell — all of whom had missed McCaw's hat-trick performance — but Canterbury, too, had much to play for. The game would be the final act in Canterbury colours for Hansen (who was off to coach Wales) and for the Scotland-bound Blackadder, who had signed a three-year contract with the Edinburgh Reivers.

Mains's Southern Men typically hadn't read the script, and at halftime of the final an upset was on the cards. Otago led 16–6 at the break before Canterbury's Blackadder-inspired forwards took charge and clinched the province's first NPC title since 1997. Within nine minutes of the restart, Otago's advantage — courtesy of tries to Brendan Laney and Sam Harding — was over; the Cantabs were back in front. Tries to Justin Marshall and Nathan Mauger,

Steve Hansen and Todd Blackadder — pictured here after masterminding the 2001 NPC win — were instrumental in the early development of Richie McCaw.

coupled with Andrew Mehrtens missing just one shot at goal and banging over a vital late dropped goal, saw Canterbury home 30–19.

For his part McCaw had put in a good shift, and Blackadder was again moved to tip the flanker for a big future. McCaw was so special, in fact, that Blackadder called for the 'handle with care' approach for the World Cup-winning member of the New Zealand Under-19s in 1999. 'If ever you're looking for the perfect number seven, which I'm sure we are, he's got to be earmarked, that boy. We've got to look long-term with a guy like him. We've got to say "we've got this amazing talent here, we've got to look out for him". Of all the players I've seen over the years . . . he's just head and shoulders above everyone I've seen lately. When you watch his game, he's got so many skills. He's a great runner with the ball and a good passer. We've had guys who have been good on the ground, but not so good at running or passing. He seems to have all those skills, which make him a complete footballer. He's just so young and keen, I believe he's going to be New Zealand's answer.'

The All Blacks of the day had a new coach. John Mitchell had just taken over from Wayne Smith, who'd lost his stomach for the top job after a heartbreaking loss to Australia in the Tri-Nations championship. Mitchell was due to name his first All Blacks team the morning following the final. And, incredibly, less than three months after coming to prominence on a national scale, McCaw's name was being mentioned as contender for the tour of Ireland, Scotland and Argentina. The way Blackadder had been talking on the night of the final, some wondered whether he had any 'inside' information. Was it really possible that McCaw would join the likes of Wilson Whineray, Kel Tremain, Andy Dalton, Craig Green, Robbie and Bruce Deans, Greg Somerville and Scott Robertson as Lincoln alumni to have worn the famous black jersey?

RICHIE McCaw must have wondered what type of circus he'd stepped into. When John Mitchell confirmed that McCaw had been selected for the end-of-year tour, controversy was never far away from the team's door. In any other year, McCaw's whirlwind rise would have been front-page news. In 2001, it wasn't. The front pages of newspapers up and down the country were dominated by news of the axing of All Black greats Christian Cullen and Jeff Wilson, as well as a former captain, Taine Randell. And when Brad Thorn — the former Broncos, Queensland and Kangaroos league star — turned down his selection, there was little chance of any newcomer dominating the news the way they normally do around the naming of All Black squads.

When those media storms eventually passed,

Josh Kronfeld, a childhood hero of Richie McCaw's, was one of McCaw's harshest critics when he was selected for the All Blacks in 2001. Kronfeld is pictured with Jeff Wilson after their 2000 Super 12 semifinal loss to the Crusaders.

another All Black great, this time Josh Kronfeld, ensured McCaw was on the front pages — but not for any reason that would have been in McCaw's dreams. Kronfeld had taken over the All Blacks' reins at No. 7 from arguably the greatest openside ever to have played the game: Michael Jones. Between 1995 and 2000 Kronfeld had played 54 tests and, while he never reached the standards Jones set, he'd won the heart of the rugby nation with an unrivalled desire to put his body on the line for the old black jersey. So when Kronfeld spoke, the people listened.

A few days after McCaw had been named in the All Blacks touring party, Kronfeld used McCaw's elevation to the upper echelon of rugby as an example of the jersey he'd worn so proudly being handed out too easily. 'I haven't seen him play, but it seems incredible to me that they so easily can put number sevens in,' said Kronfeld, who was plying his trade with Leicester. 'Before him it was Marty Holah off one Super 12 season, now they've got a guy off one NPC season. Jesus, you might as well just give All Black jerseys to everybody. The fact they picked guys off one NPC season is bloody incredible. I understand McCaw has been playing well, but anyone can play well in a team that's going well, and Canterbury have been kicking ass by all accounts.'

The irony, of course, was that McCaw grew up idolizing Kronfeld. 'When I was at school, Josh was the best at that stage — and he probably still is. I thought "Gee, if I was only half as good as him I would be going all right." But I try to take a bit of everyone and make my own sort of style. I remember Michael Jones at the '87 World Cup . . . he was the best there was, and when I was at school Josh was like that, too. I always thought if you could get a little bit out of both of those guys and put it together you'd be pretty good. But it's about moulding your own style, too.' When told of Kronfeld's comments about his All Black call-up, McCaw's response showed a maturity beyond his years. 'I don't know about that,' he said, 'but I suppose the selectors thought they picked the

John Mitchell, the first All Blacks coach to select Richie McCaw, seemed like a good choice for All Blacks coach in 2001. He would, however, leave the post in disgrace two years later, after the All Blacks' World Cup semifinal loss to Australia.

right players. I've just [got] to put up my hand and make sure I am worthy to be here, and make the most of my opportunities. It's only one fella's opinion. Being an All Black — it's taken a wee bit of getting used to. I just can't wait to get out and play. At the end of the day, you've got to play rugby, so I'm mentally preparing. It is going to be a step up, but I'm looking forward to it.'

The tour marked a real shift in All Black rugby. Mitchell and his coaching co-ordinator, Robbie Deans, selected 11 new caps in their 30-man squad — the most changes in an All Blacks squad since 1974. Canterbury supplied 16 players, which was the most by any province since 14 Aucklanders were selected for the 1987 and 1991 World Cup tournaments. And for the first test in Dublin, McCaw found himself in the famous No. 7 jersey for the first time. He would start the game alongside his back-row teammates from Canterbury: Scott Robertson and Reuben Thorne. Another Canterbury young gun, Aaron Mauger, was also making his debut. This all meant that the Irish were confident they were on track for a historic first victory over the All Blacks. Indeed, Irish newspapers were running headlines they would not have written in the days of Wilson Whineray, Graham Mourie and Buck Shelford. 'Stuff of legend beckons as Kiwis look less than invincible,' the *Sunday Independent* splattered across the top of one of its sports pages. 'Ireland can put a major dent in the New Zealand legend,' *The Sunday Tribune* said. Buoyed by a 20–14 home win over England, the Irish had an air of self-belief and were far from being in awe of Mitchell's men. 'A probable test back row of Reuben Thorne, Richard McCaw and Scott Robertson doesn't have quite the same shuddering resonance of [Mike] Brewer, [Michael] Jones and [Zinzan] Brooke', Peter O'Reilly wrote in the *Tribune*.

McCaw wasn't buying into any of the pre-test hype. With just 17 first-class games under his belt, he knew enough to know that all he could do was try to keep things in perspective as he prepared for a battle with

Ireland's David Wallace. 'It's exciting, but at the end of the day you've got to make sure you're doing the business. You've got to make sure the feet are on the ground and you're ready. This game is going to be tough.'

As it turned out, McCaw dispelled any doubts as to whether he was up to test rugby with a man-of-the-match debut against the fighting Irish. He repaid the faith that Mitchell and Deans had shown in him by climbing back into a torrid test after taking some big Irish tackles early on. 'She was a hell of a game,' McCaw said after the All Blacks came back from 7–21 down to win 40–29. 'All the hits were pretty big, in the first 20 minutes they threw everything at us. Everyone talks about it being a big step up. It was a hell of a step up . . . the first 20 minutes were gone before I knew it. I thought "Crikey, I've got to do something here." It didn't help that they were scoring points, either. It's a big learning curve for myself and the team. The big

Tana Umaga and the All Blacks came from 7–21 down to beat Ireland 40–19: Richie McCaw's first game in black.

thing is not to panic, because if you start to panic then things go real bad. Once we got into the game and started holding the ball, it came right.'

Mitchell, never one to go overboard about individuals, was 'happy' with his openside flanker, who was able to steal ball from Ireland in the second half, setting in motion a crucial try to wing Jonah Lomu. 'We put faith in him from day one,' Mitchell said. 'Richie probably had an indifferent start, but it just shows the calibre of the kid: he never let it get to him. I think we'll see more of this lad.' Robertson, his roommate, was chuffed for McCaw. He wrapped his arm around McCaw after the test and said: 'He's a bloody good boy. I'm just happy for the new boys, like Aaron Mauger and Richie, that

It took a while, but eventually the All Blacks — led by Tana Umaga — proved too good for Scotland.

we won, because [their careers] could have been tainted pretty early. One game doesn't make your career and they made a couple of mistakes, but when it counted they came through.'

McCaw impressed again in his second test against Scotland in Edinburgh. While the All Blacks' front row struggled, the back row worked well together, and were instrumental in creating good ball to turn a 18–6 scoreline with 10 minutes of the test to go into a 37–6 win, with late tries to Tana Umaga, Mark Robinson and Jonah Lomu.

While the famed grounds in Dublin and Edinburgh were noteworthy ones at which to play his first two tests, there was a feeling that McCaw and the young All Blacks in the squad would be tested like never before in the tour's last game at the River Plate Stadium in Buenos Aires. Argentina was a formidable foe on home soil, and with McCaw joined in the test line-up by the relatively inexperienced Aaron Mauger,

Mark Robinson and Ben Blair, the test was always going to be some eye-opener. And the coach knew it. 'Without doubt it's a factor, but New Zealand rugby will be better for this tour,' he said. 'But we need to know about these guys. They'll be better rugby players for it.'

The All Blacks would win a nail-biter 24–20, thanks to a last-minute try from Scott Robertson. The crucial seven-pointer, allied to Jonah Lomu's tackle-busting first-half touchdown, cancelled out two gift tries that All Black errors had handed to the Pumas. And with Andrew Mehrtens landing five of his seven shots at goal, the record of New Zealand sides never having lost to Argentina was maintained, just. The All Blacks' performance was listless, however, and their handling abysmal. Despite pledging to pull players — even the captain — if they did not perform, Mitchell kept his substitutes shackled for most of the match. It was the worst performance of the three tests on tour, but

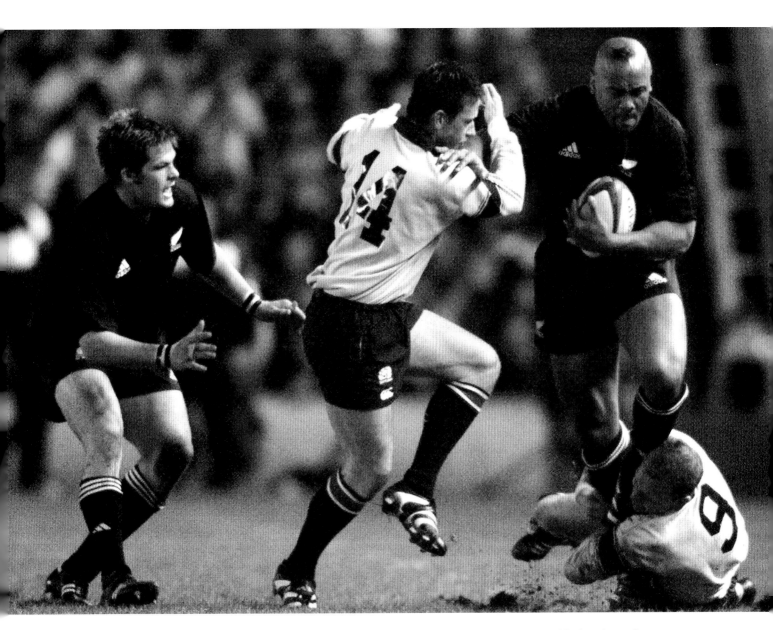

Jonah Lomu on the burst against Scotland as Richie McCaw does his best to keep pace with the giant wing.

two players shined through the mire: Lomu's try was vintage, and McCaw had another outstanding game.

While the accolades flowed for McCaw, the player himself was more concerned with what lay ahead in 2002. He might have played three tests for the All Blacks, but he was yet to test himself against the best in the Southern Hemisphere. He would get his chance with the Crusaders in the Super 12. 'It's pretty tough rugby, but I haven't been there so I don't really know what it's like,' he said before the season kick-off. 'So I'm going to have to be ready for every game and treat it like playing a test match each week.' McCaw knew the real measure of his ability would come against world-class flankers like Brumbies and Wallabies ace George Smith, the Waratahs' Phil Waugh, and rugged Stormers loosie Corné Krige. Everywhere he looked, he knew he would be confronted by test-strength opposition. 'I'm really looking forward to playing against those sorts of guys. It's great to measure yourself against someone like that. They're all pretty different players and they all have their strengths. George Smith played really well for the Wallabies, and Phil Waugh's almost as good. But there are players all over the show, so I don't think you can single anyone out — they're all pretty tough. I just want to go out, when I get a chance, and keep performing as best I can. I just want to make sure I enjoy it.'

McCaw's attitude matched that of his Crusaders coach, who did his best to keep any hype surrounding the 21-year-old to a minimum. 'The honeymoon is over, I guess, for Richie, but I'm sure he will get his head around it,' Robbie Deans said. 'He's a very intelligent sort of player and he won't get carried away with anything. He's got a lot of rugby under his belt already, and now he's involved in the Super 12 which is something new for him. I'm sure he's capable of negotiating the terrain ahead and handling the challenges that come his way.' Deans said McCaw faced the same pathway as any young player: he had to continue improving, continue adding to his game, and at the same time handle the pressure that went with being an incumbent All Black. 'He's sensible enough to know that you can only deal with the task in front of you. At the moment that's to play well for the Crusaders. Anything else, like playing for the All Blacks, is so far ahead it's just not worth considering.'

What were 'so far ahead' in the 2002 season were Deans's men. After finishing 10th the previous season, they would go through the season unbeaten, recording 13 consecutive wins, and in the process dishing up one of the all-time great displays when they tore a star-studded New South Wales side to shreds, winning 96–19. A week after that game — the last of the round robin — McCaw stole the show in the Crusaders' 34–23 semifinal win against Laurie Mains's Highlanders. He crashed over for the try that clinched the red-and-blacks' place in the final against the Brumbies. McCaw struck just as the Highlanders were clawing their way back into the game after Jeff Wilson slipped through for a try that closed the gap to 21–16. Typically, there was no hint of panic in the Crusaders ranks, and seven minutes later McCaw steered them to safety. The Crusaders forwards maintained their composure and took charge of proceedings, setting up a series of drives that negated the Highlanders' spread defence. McCaw, who had made a series of big tackles and turned over critical ball at the breakdowns, featured twice in the attack before crashing over for the try that restored his team's 12-point lead at a key time in the game.

In the final against the Brumbies, the Crusaders were helped by the Australians' coach David Nucifora tactically playing into the home side's hands by trying to take them on physically. It backfired, as the Crusaders constantly counter-attacked from deep and stuck strictly to their pre-match plan of keeping the ball in hand as they cruised to a 31–13 victory.

Jonah Lomu is tackled by Diego Albanese in the All Blacks' 24–20 win in 2001.

'I just want to go out, when I get a chance,
and keep performing as best I can.
I just want to make sure I enjoy it.'

McCaw's place in the first All Blacks squad of the year was never in doubt. Well, not once he'd sorted out his mental approach to the game. At the beginning of 2002 he'd been unsure if he'd ever wear the All Black jersey again after his first tour. 'Before the Super 12, I had a fear that I would be the guy that burst onto the scene only to disappear again,' he said. 'I realized that it was too easy for me to stand out in 2001 because no one knew who I was. [Then] things were different. People knew me. They knew my game. It didn't help that after the tour there was a lot of hype around about me. I was apprehensive . . . and I played like it. The first couple of weeks of the Super 12 weren't great, because I tried to be a hero and do something special every time. I had to have a yarn to the coaches, because I ended up doing nothing properly. They told me to go out and do my job. They reminded me that an All Black is someone who does his job every week, not just some weeks. Once I got my head around that — and it helped that the team went well — I was able to do my job and things got better as the season went on.'

Steve Hansen, one of the coaches McCaw had turned to in the past, had been impressed when McCaw began to second-guess his approach. 'I would rather a young player question himself than think that after one All Blacks tour he has arrived. Richie is intelligent and mature, but at the same time he is still a young man. We talked about the need to continue to be Richie McCaw — we stressed the importance of not losing touch with who he was. Just because he was an All Black didn't give him the licence to change his nature or his values. As a coach you are always concerned about how players will deal with the pressure and the added attention. We asked him to focus on the enjoyment side of being a good player and to remember the reasons why he first started playing the game. His humility makes him a pleasure to be around and a pleasure to work with. It is that humbleness and the fact that he felt like he did at the start of the Super 12 that makes him what he

ABOVE: Richie McCaw congratulates Marika Vunibaka after the Fijian scored against the Brumbies in the 2002 Super 12, which was McCaw's first full season with the Crusaders.

FOLLOWING PAGES: The Crusaders celebrate their 2002 Super 12 success — a victory that came by way of a 31–13 win against the Brumbies.

is. He is striving all the time to get better. To be better. He is never content. In any person — whether they are involved in sport or not — if they are striving to be better today than they were yesterday, then you know they are on the path to success.'

McCaw was determined, above all, to remain true to himself. 'One of the biggest fears I have is that people perceive me as getting arrogant or carried away with the success. I have seen guys get carried away and make fools of themselves, and I am very careful not to do that. I flat with guys that don't play

a lot of footie. They're in a different scene, and that helps to keep me in the real world. If I was hanging with rugby people exclusively, I would be with guys who know only rugby and, because we were together all the time, we would end up believing our own press and forget about the real world. It's hard to explain . . . it's a fear I had and I hope I haven't changed too much. Life is a little bit different, but you just have to make sure that your core values don't change. In that sense, Canterbury is the perfect environment for me. Being around so many good players helps as well. If I was somewhere else around the country, as a guy who had played [some] tests, I would have been a senior guy. But at Canterbury I am still very much the new boy in the team and that keeps it real as well. If you got big-headed in our team environment, you wouldn't last very long.'

McCaw was named in the first All Blacks squad of 2002, along with the rest of the Crusaders pack, for the tests against Italy, Ireland and Fiji. The biggest benefactor was Reuben Thorne, by now the All Blacks captain after Mitchell's first choice, Anton Oliver, had been ruled out with an injury. Such was the Crusaders' dominance in the Super 12 that Mitchell also found room for seven Crusaders backs in the squad. And sure enough, in the two tests against Ireland, 13 Crusaders played in Dunedin (Blues wing Doug Howlett and the Hurricanes' Tana Umaga being the odd men out), and 14 in Auckland, when the Hurricanes' Jonah Lomu was the only non-red-and-black in the run-on side.

McCaw, who played in both of the Irish tests — 15–6 and 40–8 wins, respectively — had established himself as the number-one openside in the squad, with Marty Holah and Sam Harding sharing the No. 7 starting duties either side of the Irish internationals.

While the country had marvelled at the rookie efforts of McCaw on his first tour at the end of the previous year, the 2002 version was bigger and better. Bigger, in that at 102kg he had added 5kg to his frame; and better, in that he had a full Super 12 season under his

Steve Hansen, who joined Wales at the end of 2001, admired McCaw's attitude towards his new-found fame from afar. 'I would rather a young player question himself than think that after one All Blacks tour he has arrived.'

belt to tune for test football. 'This series [against Ireland] has been one of the most physical I've played,' he said ahead of his first Tri-Nations experience. 'Ireland commit more than we are used to at breakdown. They pack you in, where we are used to cleaning out the breakdown and setting up our defensive lines. No. 7 is a position where you get whacked every time. Tests are a lot tighter than Super 12, and there's definitely a bit more forward contact. I was pretty sore after that Dunedin test, and my recovery was a bit slower than it has been all season coming into this game. I've put on 5 kilograms since the tour last year, and I think that's a maturing thing as much as anything. But it has helped me. You don't feel the knocks quite as much as I have done. These days you need a bit of size to compete in international rugby, but I don't want to get a whole lot bigger . . . I'll have to start looking at another position!'

Reuben Thorne took over the All Blacks captaincy in 2002.

With five tests under his belt, McCaw was beginning to feel comfortable in his new lofty surroundings. 'I went pretty much from the NPC to test rugby, and my Super 12 base has helped this year. It was a case of having to get up every week for big games. In test rugby you have to work hard for absolutely everything. I feel I've learned a lot since my start on last year's tour. The big thing is to take a step every time we play. You are not going to be perfect, but it's a matter of keeping building and achieving something each time we play . . . a couple of things each game and you get better and better.'

The All Blacks — despite being unbeaten under Mitchell — needed to up the ante before the next test against Australia. New Zealand hadn't held the

Bledisloe Cup since Rod Macqueen's team had run off with it after inflicting three consecutive defeats on John Hart's All Blacks in 1998. If Mitchell was going to achieve his goal of wresting it back, his team would need to make the most of home-ground advantage in the opening game. That it was in Christchurch was an obvious boost, given the number of Crusaders in the team. And 12 of them — Caleb Ralph, Mark Robinson, Aaron Mauger, Andrew Mehrtens and Justin Marshall in the backs, and forwards Scott Robertson, McCaw, Reuben Thorne, Chris Jack, Greg Somerville, Mark Hammett and Dave Hewett — were named to start the test alongside 'outsiders' Christian Cullen, Doug Howlett and Simon Maling.

The high contingent of locals certainly helped as the All Blacks won the first try-less test at Christchurch 12–6: four penalties to Mehrtens getting them home on a typically cold, wet, wintery Christchurch night. It was a win built on guts and determination, and provided the young McCaw with a career highlight. 'When you're a little kid, you dream of playing for the All Blacks in a big test match like the Bledisloe Cup. It doesn't come much bigger than that.' The greatest sign from the test was the courage that Mitchell's team showed when centre Mark Robinson was sin-binned for the last 10 minutes. 'Everyone dug in,' said McCaw. 'That's probably the value of this team when it comes to defending the line. We dug real deep and got away with it. It's going to help us in the future for the belief we can do it. The biggest thing is we believe in each other to make those tackles.'

McCaw put in his best shift for the All Blacks the following weekend in Wellington, when he helped the team to a 41–20 win against the Springboks. Chris Laidlaw, a former All Black writing in *The Dominion*, had joined the ever-growing Richie McCaw Appreciation Society. 'Loose forwards Scott Robertson, Richie McCaw and Reuben Thorne were outstanding, with the team's "fourth" loosie Justin Marshall close behind,' wrote Laidlaw. 'Robertson, who spent more time going back than forward in the early tests of the year, was good against the Aussies but better against the Boks. He tackled strongly, broke the advantage line, set hooker Mark Hammett up for a try and finished the game in style with a try of his own. McCaw was equally impressive with his scavenging skills superb. Whenever the All Blacks needed someone to snap up the loose ball to keep the momentum going, McCaw was the man. McCaw ripping the ball free from a ruck in the All Blacks' in-goal area after the Boks drove

Wallabies flanker George Smith is tackled by Andrew Mehrtens while Richie McCaw halts the progress of Stephen Larkham as the All Blacks open their 2002 Tri-Nations account with a 12–6 win in Christchurch.

across the line was one of the match highlights for me.'

George Smith — the Wallabies breakaway — was impressed, too. As McCaw prepared to try to play the role of hero in the team's next outing in Sydney, Smith heaped praise on the Tri-Nations newbie. 'Richie McCaw is a tough customer, as well as the other two back-rowers,' said Smith. 'He has shown in the Super 12 that he can be dominant in the breakdown. If we can shut down the back row and [lock] Chris Jack as well, it would be pretty good for us. Both the All Blacks and the Springboks are very intense, and we can't go into one game thinking one is going to be less than the other. But games against the All Blacks are very fast and it's not going to be any different this weekend.'

For his part, McCaw was enjoying his new rivalries with Smith and the Boks' Joe van Niekerk. 'Playing against van Niekerk and Smith has been a hell of a challenge,' McCaw said. 'I reckon they're both the best in the world at the moment, and they're both still young. Against van Niekerk in Wellington we had a hell of a scrap for the ball. I can see them both being around for a while yet, and it'll be great to set up long-term rivalries. Every time I come up against them I certainly don't want to come off second best.'

In Stadium Australia's then stirring three-year history of hosting rugby tests , the Wallabies have felt defeat at the venue just once in seven tests. Most of the magic had come from the Wallabies. The only time their golden run was punctured was in 2000, when Jonah Lomu tiptoed down the sideline to secure a 39–35 win for the All Blacks. The other conjuring acts have favoured the Wallabies, like their 2001 series win against the Lions and Toutai Kefu's try against the All Blacks to crown John Eales's farewell from international rugby.

The stage was set for another epic, and the upset against the world champions looked on when McCaw scored a 47th-minute try — his first for his country — to give the All Blacks an 11–8 lead. An Andrew Mehrtens' penalty pushed them out to 14–8 with 17 minutes to go. The Bledisloe looked like it was finally coming home, before a late rally from the Aussies saw them storm home 16–14, courtesy of a Mat Rogers try and a last-minute penalty from Matt Burke. 'I'm pretty gutted and the guys are pretty shattered in there,' McCaw said after the game. 'We've got to look at it like we didn't play that badly, we put ourselves into a position to win and it was just one call that didn't go our way. We made one mistake that cost us the game. As gutted as we are, we realize we didn't play that badly. You've got to give credit to these Wallaby teams. They never give up and they showed that tonight. We've got to match them next year, I suppose. There's nothing between these teams. Both tests could have gone either way, it's just a pity it didn't go ours tonight.'

McCaw was diplomatic when questioned on the effort of South African referee Andre Watson. McCaw's role puts him under the glare more than most, especially at the contentious breakdown areas. 'Each ref is different, and you have got to make sure you adapt. At times, no matter what the ref called, I'm always going to think I'm in the right. The ref has got to make a call . . . it's a hard area to ref and you've just got to play to him. He was the same for both teams, and that's all you ask for. A couple of times I thought I was harshly dealt to, and probably they did, too. I've got no qualms with the ref.' And that included the gut-wrenching last penalty that cost New Zealand a famous victory. 'I suppose it was legitimate, but who knows? It could have gone either way. The ref has got to make a call and he did.'

This diplomacy was another indication of McCaw's captaincy credentials. Not all of the All Blacks could be so controlled in the test's aftermath: All Black first-five Andrew Mehrtens was scathing of Watson, saying he should be 'ashamed' of his performance. 'I'm not sure if Australia deserved to win. We probably lost the game more so, but we were helped to lose it obviously,' he said, referring to Watson. 'He should be

Wallabies skipper George Gregan hoists the Bledisloe Cup after the All Blacks lost 16–14 in Sydney in 2002.

more ashamed than some of us should be.'

Despite the loss, the All Blacks still had the chance to claim the Tri-Nations title in Durban the following week. 'Unity is the key to our success as a team,' McCaw said. 'We all get on so well that when we go out we play for each other. It doesn't matter which province the guys come from, we all know each other and bring something different to the All Blacks' style. We just have to stay united and we'll be OK.'

And despite the loss, McCaw's star was still shining brightly. *Sunday Star Times* columnist Phil Gifford had been mightily impressed with McCaw's effort at Stadium Australia. 'Richie McCaw was astonishingly active,' wrote Gifford. 'The work-rate he managed last night was even greater than George Smith could manage for Australia. True, McCaw was penalized at times, but, as Wallabies 1991 World Cup coach Bob Dwyer is fond of noting: "Of course a loosie gets picked up for hands in the ruck. It's what you do. You wouldn't expect the bloody fullback to get caught doing that would you?" '

Someone who got caught in Durban was referee David McHugh. A crazed South African rugby fan attacked and injured the referee in front of a stunned crowd during the All Blacks' game against the Boks. The Irish ref suffered a dislocated shoulder and was forced to leave the field after Pieter van Zyl ran onto Kings Park and crash-tackled him to the ground. Van Zyl, who had managed to scale a perimeter fence and escape security guards, attacked McHugh as a scrum was being set. McCaw and Scott Robertson were the first to react as they wrestled the fan off McHugh. 'I didn't know what was going on,' McCaw said. 'I looked up, the ref got bashed into, and I saw a Bok jersey. My very first thought was "Shit, a South African player has had a crack at the ref!" You just don't know. You never expect a spectator to be out there. I just thought "Hang on, I've got to do something here." I got him down and then the South African players touched him up. I was pleased about that.' It was just one incident of many in an action-packed test that saw the All Blacks eventually get home 30–23, with Tana Umaga in sublime form directing a backline that scored all of the team's four tries. The Tri-Nations title was all but claimed, the result dependant on whether the Wallabies would beat the Boks the following weekend in Johannesburg (a game they would lose 31–33). The All Blacks were Tri-Nations champions for the first time since 1999.

McCaw, desperate to keep his dream alive, was talking about the end-of-year tour to England, France and Wales the day before the Durban test. Rumours had been circulating that Mitchell would rest a number of players from the tour as he planned his attack on the World Cup the following year. McCaw, however, was hopeful of not being one of the 'rested'. 'Whenever you get the chance to pull on an All Blacks jersey, you don't turn it down,' he said. 'It's a great honour.' Mitchell talked of taking McCaw on the tour, telling *Sunday News* he couldn't put him in 'cotton wool. We need to keep him going. He's right on top of his game, physically and technically. He's a great player. He would acknowledge there's still room for improvement, but the key for him is to continue the momentum.'

But when it came time to announce the team, McCaw's name was missing. He was in good company, though. After helping Canterbury through to the semifinals of the NPC (where they would lose to Auckland), McCaw, Greg Feek, Corey Flynn, Mark Hammett, Dave Hewett, Chris Jack, Leon MacDonald, Justin Marshall, Aaron Mauger, Norm Maxwell, Caleb Ralph, Scott Robertson, Greg Somerville and Reuben Thorne were all left out of the tour. Other All Blacks rested were Otago's Tony Brown, Byron Kelleher, Simon Maling, Tom Willis and Anton Oliver, Wellington's Jerry Collins, and North Harbour's Ron Cribb. It meant a swag of new All Blacks, including Daniel Braid, Steve Devine, Andrew Hore, Regan King, Danny Lee, Keith Lowen, Keven Mealamu, Bradley Mika, Keith Robinson, Rodney So'oialo, Ali Williams and Tony Woodcock.

The rugby nation wasn't thrilled with all the 'rotation' — a buzz word that would be reused ahead of the 2007 World Cup. But all these changes were taking place ahead of the 2003 World Cup. 'The chance to get some pre-season work under their belt [before the 2003 season] was important,' All Black No. 2 Robbie Deans said. 'They will have a better aerobic base and better strength. The public misunderstand what these guys go through. This work will not give us an advantage, but will put us back level with the other teams. Rather than tapering they will be sustaining their efforts. And looking at the big picture, that will be important to go the full distance for the World Cup.'

The All Blacks were quickly installed as the overwhelming favourites to lift the trophy in a few months' time . . .

BEFORE the World Cup year could begin, John Mitchell's under-strength All Blacks side lost to England before drawing with France and beating Wales. One of the stand-out players for the team was Marty Holah, the Waikato openside who was playing in the No. 7 jersey that Richie McCaw had donned for nine tests.

McCaw, who had been named as the International Rugby Players' Association 'newcomer of the year', was one of five finalists for the IRB Player of the Year Award — the honour eventually going to France's Fabien Galthié. But as a nominee, McCaw was flown to Europe and found himself watching the All Blacks' tests against the Tri-colours in Paris. Said McCaw: 'When I got back from the Tri-Nations [in 2002] I felt pretty good and thought that there was no way I would not go on that tour. But as the season went on, it got harder and harder. Mitch had a yarn to me and sort of said that there is a rest available here and that I should take it. It was a tough decision, but I knew deep down that if the World Cup had come around I wouldn't have been much good. I knew that I needed some time off. But, even knowing that, it was still the toughest decision that I have had ever had to make. Mitch made it a little easier by communicating with me, but watching the games . . . the old mind was racing, wondering if it had been the right thing to do. It was tough watching. [Marty] really stepped up and that [made] it even tougher for me in 2003. But Marty was always going to push me, and that's not a bad thing. If you don't have competition, you sit back and relax. He has certainly given me a little extra motivation to hit the ground running.'

Phil Gifford, the *Sunday Star Times* scribe, was in Paris and witnessed first-hand an incident which left a long-lasting impression on him. '[Richie McCaw] was sitting in Paris next to a New Zealand official who couldn't resist noting the outstanding form of Waikato openside flanker Marty Holah. It's a measure of McCaw's decency that he kept smiling through gritted teeth, even after the 11th or 12th shouted reference by his companion to the sheer brilliance of the Waikato man. How keen do you think McCaw is to get on the paddock this year?'

The answer was 'plenty keen'. Not only was McCaw

Marty Holah did his best to displace Richie McCaw from his regular All Blacks spot with this try against Ireland at Eden Park.

determined to repeat the previous season's Super 12 win, but — like every man playing for one of the five New Zealand franchises — he was very much focused on the World Cup to be held in Australia after the Tri-Nations. 'With the All Blacks [in 2002], John Mitchell told us pretty early on that, while he wanted us to win every game we played — like every All Blacks team should — he said that everything we do from now on, regardless of who is playing and who isn't, is about winning the World Cup. Every game we play is one step in that direction. Now, after the tour, there are 45 guys who have had a taste of playing for the All Blacks and who will be dreaming of playing at the World Cup. If we can get the best out of every one of those people I can't see any reason why we can't win it. There is a team of New Zealanders who can be selected and win the Cup. It's up to me to make sure I am a part of that side.'

McCaw would be a part of what was billed as the 'ultimate All Blacks trial' when the Crusaders travelled to Eden Park to play the Blues in the Super 12 final in May, five months ahead of the All Blacks' opening World Cup game. The Crusaders had qualified with their normal efficient style of rugby, which was built around a never-say-die forward pack and a backline that was benefitting from the skills of Super 12 newbies like Aaron Mauger and Dan Carter, who had combined to keep Andrew Mehrtens's appearances down to just three starts in the competition. In contrast, the Blues were being directed by Carlos Spencer, his confidence boosted by his inclusion on the 2002 All Blacks tour. He, too, had some young talent to feed — Mils Muliaina and Joe Rokocoko included — as the Blues set a new standard of excellence for sublime backline rugby.

On the night it would be the Blues who would triumph, 21–17. McCaw won rave reviews for his tireless contribution during the epic, but ultimately it was the Blues' defence — as they snuffed out late try-scoring opportunities to Carter and Leon MacDonald — that decided the resting destination for the Super 12 trophy.

It was a deserved victory for the Auckland-based side, and, despite the Crusaders nation being stung by the defeat (they'd won four of the last five finals), not even the folks based in Christchurch could feel too gloomy, as the overall All Blacks picture looked great — at least until the squad for the first tests of the year was named and All Black legends Mehrtens and Christian Cullen were missing. The squad for the domestic games against England, Wales and France did include five new names: Muliaina, Rokocoko, Carter, Ma'a Nonu and Brad Thorn. Mitchell, clearly, was comfortable with leaving out the Big Two. 'To me, the All Blacks is about a team of excellence,' Mitchell said. 'When you have to make tough calls and leave good players out, that shows the level that exists in New Zealand.'

That level of excellence would be tested in Wellington for the year's first test. The England team brought to New Zealand by Clive Woodward was nothing like the teams that had toured in previous years. This was a full-strength side — men with big reputations, like Jason Robinson, Jonny Wilkinson, Matt Dawson, Lawrence Dallaglio, Neil Back, Martin Johnson, Richard Hill and Jason Leonard, all looking to strike a psychological blow against the World Cup favourites ahead of the tournament.

They would do that, and arguably more, in spectacular circumstances during the 15–13 win. At one stage, England was down to 13 men — two forwards having been sin-binned — but they still managed to hold out the All Blacks' forward pack. If there was a moral victory to be had, the All Blacks could at least claim that they scored the game's only try — to Doug Howlett — but certainly the English left

New Zealand's shores with their confidence at an all-time high, while the start to New Zealand's World Cup campaign had been ugly. McCaw offered 'no excuses' to reporters after the game, while Mitchell conceded that England had made a point: 'Psychologically, it's fantastic for England,' he said. 'But I don't think this loss at this stage is damaging for us. We will improve, there is no doubt about that. We showed signs of a lack of cohesion and we lacked composure at times. We have to learn, and we learnt the hard way tonight. We lacked rhythm and our attack got isolated at times.'

McCaw didn't immediately get the chance to avenge his first loss in a black jersey; Marty Holah was handed the No. 7 jersey for the straightforward 55–3 win against a depleted Welsh outfit at Hamilton. McCaw was recalled to the team, along with the rest of the 'first-teamers', for the clash against an under-strength French side a week later in Christchurch. If the squad rotation was bothering him, McCaw wasn't letting on. 'I've heard people say we should put the strongest XV out every time but, to be quite honest, sometimes the strongest XV could actually be with a few changes,' McCaw said. 'There could be 14 tests for us this year, and there's no way 15 guys can play all 14 and be at the peak of their game in November.'

The All Blacks would see off the French 31–23, but it was hardly convincing. After Joe Rokocoko had scored three tries in the game's first 30 minutes — and helped the All Blacks to a 19–3 lead — the French slowly worked their way back into the contest. The lack of a killer instinct and general flair had many observers worried. *Sunday Star Times* contributor Michael Laws summed up the feeling of many in one much-quoted sentence: 'If we meet them at the World Cup, it's simple: stack the ABs with Richie McCaw and 14 Islanders and we'll murder them.'

Others pointed to captain Reuben Thorne as being the All Blacks' weak link. Former All Blacks captain Stu Wilson was adamant that Thorne — coined 'The Invisable Man' by his critics — be replaced by McCaw in time for the World Cup. 'It's just not happening for Thorne at the moment,' he said. 'I'm a huge Tana fan, but I feel coach John Mitchell would be more comfortable with McCaw leading the outfit. I know it's a huge call. But it's the type of thing that could galvanize the team and spark them into something dynamic. McCaw is THE outstanding player in the side, and he's had leadership experience with the Under-21 side. He's inspirational and commands respect. It's a matter of "when" not "if" he becomes captain, so why not now? It doesn't matter if you're 22 or 32 — if you're good enough you're old enough.'

The New Zealand Listener's Joseph Romanos concurred. 'My pick for captain would be McCaw,' he wrote. 'He is already taking on such a role of responsibility within the team that he seems a natural captain. Wilson Whineray and Graham Mourie led teams in their early 20s. McCaw offers the same sort of quality.'

McCaw certainly showed leadership ahead of the All Blacks' opening Tri-Nations test against the Springboks in Pretoria when he told reporters he didn't think he'd been doing his job properly in his opening tests of the year. 'We didn't get enough clean ball at the breakdowns [against England and France]. It's about being more composed at the breakdown and dealing better with players lying around the ball. We've got to work on that. The rest of the guys have been there: Jerry [Collins], Rodney [So'oialo] and Reuben [Thorne].'

Mitchell wanted two players — McCaw and whoever was playing No. 8 — to get to every breakdown quickly and to be accurate when they did. It was Thorne's job to bring up the second wave of forwards to clean out opposition and make life easier for the halfback to clear. McCaw said that the first two guys had not been accurate enough. 'That's why the ball's been slowed up and why people are getting the perception that there's no one there doing the job. All it needs is the first two guys doing the job properly, then it doesn't matter what the rest do. International sides

The All Blacks' World Cup year in 2003 got off to a disastrous start when they crashed to a loss against England at Wellington, despite Richie McCaw stopping a Jonny Wilkinson burst on this particular occasion.

take it right to the limit in terms of playing offside and slowing it down. In test rugby, the time period you've got to get the ball is a lot shorter than in Super 12. You may only get two or three goes at the ball in a game, and that could be the difference. I sometimes get frustrated at what refs do, but it's a tough one, because what the English do and what the French do — and they're very good at it — is pushing right at the limit and you think "Oh, he's going to penalize them" and they don't and your chance is gone.'

McCaw, then 22, had been a lot more prominent with ball in hand — the result of hard yards in training — and it was something his coaches had picked up on. 'We had a look at how many times I've carried the ball and it's not a whole lot more than usual. It is something I've worked on a hell of a lot, though. So maybe I've just been seen out in the open a little bit more than usual. In the past it hasn't been a strength of mine. It's just little things: being able to be able to beat a man and stuff like that. At the same time, I've got to do that while I'm doing all the sort of stuff that got me in the team in the first place. If I let that slip, I'm not doing my job.'

The All Blacks responded to the criticism that had been levelled at them with an extraordinary fortnight. They inflicted a 52–16 win on the Springboks, and seven days later they were in Sydney putting the Wallabies to the sword 50–21. Posting back-to-back half-centuries against South Africa and Australia was unheard of. The mood, not surprisingly, had changed very quickly. The clamour about Christian Cullen had been dulled by Mils Muliaina; the call for Andrew Mehrtens's return repelled by Carlos Spencer and Aaron Mauger.

With a win in Sydney meaning that the Bledisloe Cup would be New Zealand's if the All Blacks were able to triumph in Auckland, Mitchell rested his two premier forwards, lock Chris Jack and McCaw, for the intervening test against South Africa in Dunedin. The game would be won 19–11, and, while the win wasn't convincing, the very fact that the test was won meant that Mitchell's men could claim both the Bledisloe and the Tri-Nations championship with a victory at Eden Park — the pressure of the occasion similar to what the team would face in the do-or-die atmosphere of the World Cup.

A 21–17 win confirmed their favouritism for the gold trophy as they wrestled the Bledisloe from their arch-rivals for the first time in five years. The win was built on a staunch defence: one that had conceded only three tries in four tests. For the record, Mitchell's men

had scored 26 tries in the same time period. As the team huddled in the middle of the park after the final whistle, McCaw, an ice-pack strapped to a thigh, limped heavily to the sideline. As the crowd chanted his name, he raised his arm in the air, fist clenched, in salute. He had never seen the Bledisloe Cup up close before, and there was no denying what the win meant to him. 'In 1988 I watched that game [on tape] over and over. Now, to get it, win it, is outstanding,' he said.

Romanos drew a line between McCaw's heroic efforts in defence at Eden Park and the 22-year-old joining the royal line of New Zealand openside flankers. The openside flanker position seems to suit the New Zealand physique and psyche. Certainly the All Blacks have been served over the past century by some champion openside flankers, and McCaw belongs in their company. Before the First World War, Auckland loosie Charlie Seeling, known as Bronco, was regarded as the best forward in the world. Between the wars, that mantle passed to another New Zealander, Maurice Brownlie, who had speed, strength, foresight and competitiveness — the attributes we seek in our top flankers today. Since the Second World War, the All Black openside flanker has invariably been a wonderful player. Bill Clark, Kel Tremain, Waka Nathan, Ian Kirkpatrick, Graham Mourie, Michael Jones, Josh Kronfeld, and now McCaw. It's some list.

'But are we over-hyping McCaw?' asked Romanos. 'I don't think so. It's difficult to think of an area in which he doesn't excel. Hennie Muller, the Springbok flanker who so devastated the 1949 All Blacks, used to talk about "running the line". He would tackle the first-five, get up and smash the second-five, then the centre. On a good day he liked to have a go at the winger, too. McCaw is starting to do the same. Against Australia, he several times made two bruising tackles in one phase of play and once he pulled off three. When there was all the fuss a few months ago about who might lead the All Blacks, those who closely follow rugby tipped McCaw. It seemed remarkable that a player

ABOVE: Finally! The All Blacks won the Bledisloe Cup prior to the 2003 World Cup for the first time since John Hart's All Blacks lost it in 1998.

RIGHT: McCaw — pictured in support of Reuben Thorne — was instrumental in the 21–17 victory at Eden Park.

who made his test debut only in 2001 and before this season had played just nine tests should be even considered. But, just as Wilson Whineray and Graham Mourie were obvious captains at a young age, so is McCaw. Already his leadership is evident on the field. He is forever organizing the defence, setting it up at critical times. When we analyse McCaw's contribution, he scores high marks in speed, tackling, ability to impose himself physically, support play and ball skills. My test for McCaw is this: can you remember him doing anything silly? He is such a gifted and intelligent player he has no need to take short-cuts or infringe, and instinctively knows what is the smartest play.'

The win at Eden Park nailed the fate of superstars Christian Cullen and Andrew Mehrtens. And two former captains — Anton Oliver and Taine Randell — also had their hopes knifed by the clinical All Blacks display. Mitchell's squad would include only minor surprises: the inclusion of the Blues' No. 7 Daniel Braid to back up McCaw and Holah, and the addition of Canterbury's Corey Flynn behind Keven Mealamu and Mark Hammett at hooker. The squad was: backs — Mils Muliaina, Leon MacDonald, Ben Blair, Doug Howlett, Joe Rokocoko, Caleb Ralph, Tana Umaga, Ma'a Nonu, Aaron Mauger, Daniel Carter, Carlos Spencer, Justin Marshall, Steve Devine and Byron Kelleher; forwards — Jerry Collins, Rodney So'oialo, McCaw, Holah, Braid, Reuben Thorne, Ali Williams, Chris Jack, Brad Thorn, Greg Somerville, Kees Meeuws, Dave Hewett, Carl Hoeft, Mealamu, Hammett and Flynn.

Before the team had left to set up at their Melbourne base, lock Ali Williams had cried out of training sessions with an injured ankle. This meant that Brad Thorn came in for him for the opening game against Italy, and he was one of the star performers as the All Blacks cruised to a 70–7 victory. The win was soured by an injury to centre Tana Umaga, who hurt his knee in a 21st-minute collision with first-five Carlos Spencer. Umaga would not return to the line-up for the duration of the tournament, despite reports after the World Cup

suggesting he was fit to play from the semifinal stages on. As a result, Leon MacDonald, a fullback, would play at centre — four years after a similar experiment with Christian Cullen had backfired with the All Blacks losing to France in the semifinals.

McCaw was benched for the tournament's second game — against Canada — as Mitchell made nine changes to his team to face the minnows. Not surprisingly, the team lacked cohesion against the North Americans, although they strolled to a 68–6 win. McCaw was missing again for the Tongan game (won 91–7) before returning to the fray for the final group game against Steve Hansen's Welsh side. He was given the No. 7 jersey, but many commentators had suggested he play at No. 8 given the poor form of Rodney So'oialo at the back of the scrum. McCaw had played some minutes in the position against Italy and off the bench against Canada. 'Playing at No. 8 is a new thing to me,' McCaw said before the game. 'I haven't had a crack there for a while — I used to play there when I was at school. Right through the season with the All Blacks Mitch has had me doing a bit of work at No. 8 and No. 6. I've been really enjoying it. I am pretty happy at No. 7. But if I get pushed to No. 8 by someone else, then I'd be happy to go there. With three opensides in the mix, they have targeted me to play the other two positions. So if they wanted to have a specialist No. 7 cover on the bench, then I can cover the other loose forward positions.'

As well as the make-up of the All Blacks, the other burning issue at the tournament was the differences in rule interpretations between Southern and Northern Hemisphere referees. McCaw told reporters: 'There are a few subtle differences. The Northern Hemisphere refs are a little quicker to blow things up. You just have to work with the refs.' One area of contention was the breakdown, and the winner of confusion seemed to be England, who relied on its big pack to get go forward and its No. 7, Neil Back, to play the role of linkman. South African No. 6, Corné Krige, Australia's Phil Waugh, and McCaw seemed to be disadvantaged.

'Back's not as much of a threat because he's more worried about making tackles and slowing ball down, whereas I go about trying to win the ball,' McCaw said. 'Krige and Waugh are similar [to me]. At the breakdown, the odds are they're going to be having a crack at the ball. We have to be pretty careful and make sure we're there at the same time and don't give them that chance. Northern Hemisphere teams aren't worried about that. They'll wait for two or three of them to pile in and try to drive you out of the way, and either slow your ball down or push you off it.'

The game against Wales was perfectly timed for the All Blacks, who needed a tough match before entering the finals phase of the competition. Welsh coach Steve Hansen did the New Zealanders no favours, though, as he left out first-stringers — the injured stars Iestyn Harris, Martyn Williams, Kevin Morgan, Dwayne Peel, Ceri Sweeney, Dafydd Jones, Gethin Jenkins and

John Mitchell and his assistant coach Robbie Deans face the press during the All Blacks' 2003 World Cup campaign.

Gareth Llewellyn. In hindsight it was probably a good thing that Hansen didn't field his strongest side, as his 'B' team was good enough to give Mitchell's team a real fright. The 53–37 scoreline was flattering for the All Blacks. It was the fourth highest points the All Blacks have conceded in tests; behind the 42 by France in 2000, the 43 the French scored in the 1999 World Cup semifinal, and the 46 by South Africa in Johannesburg in 2000. Wales led for much of the second half after a run of 24 unanswered points, and were hauled in only because the All Blacks were fitter and more used to the fast pace of the game. They finished with eight tries, two each for wings Joe Rokocoko and Doug Howlett, while centre Leon MacDonald also scored

and contributed a valuable 13 points with the boot.

The defensive lapses meant there were plenty of nerves ahead of the quarterfinal against the Springboks in Melbourne. The team's flashy backs had hogged the headlines, but the forwards knew that the set-pieces held the key to success or failure. 'If your scrum doesn't hold up, you are history — and the same at lineout time,' McCaw said. 'If you let their forward pack get on top of you, they've got some good backs, but you've got to match them up front. At times we've matched them, but we've never really dominated them, I don't think. There hasn't been a lot in a lot of the games. Maybe this week could be the difference between the forward packs.' McCaw also targeted a critical area where the All Blacks needed to show a collective improvement: defence. 'We let ourselves down really [against Wales]. The Welsh were very good at taking the opportunities they got,

Joe Rokocoko — the great All Blacks wing — was at the top of his game as the All Blacks slipped past Wales in the World Cup.

and I guess the Springboks will do the same. If we do that again, they will punish us.'

The All Blacks responded to McCaw's rallying cry, beating their old foe 29–9. Holding the Boks try-less on such a big stage was something to be proud of. McCaw, his back-row mates Jerry Collins and Reuben Thorne, hooker Keven Mealamu, and halfback Justin Marshall had been the standouts as the All Blacks booked a Sydney semifinal showdown against host Australia. 'Many people have underestimated the ability of our forward pack and sometimes they don't get the rewards they are due, but they were superb tonight,' Mitchell said. And Mealamu, too, was saying all the right things to leave New Zealanders in a

Keven Mealamu was one of the All Blacks' three try scorers as they took care of their quarterfinal opponents South Africa in Melbourne 29–9. The others to touch down were Leon MacDonald and Joe Rokocoko.

confident frame of mind ahead of the semifinal. 'It's a great feeling out there,' he said. 'The boys really worked for each other, and it showed. We played against a very physical pack, and I think the scoreline didn't really show how hard we had to work. They are a proud side and they never gave up — neither did we.'

It wasn't only the All Blacks who had been impressed by their performance. Words like 'astonishing', 'magic' and 'outrageous' were used by the world's media. David Kirk, the only All Blacks captain to lift the Webb Ellis Cup, said he always thought the All Blacks had the skill to win the cup. 'Now I really believe they will win it.' Even the Aussies were running scared. If the Wallabies — dubbed 'The Wobblies' by Melbourne's *Sunday Age* — played like they did against Scotland in their quarterfinal, they'd be 'bushwhacked' by the All Blacks, said Sydney's *Sun Herald*.

Ultimately, though, it all counted for nothing. Once the semifinal kicked off there were worrying signs for New Zealand: Chris Jack under-used in a struggling lineout, McCaw missing tackles, static players hammered in midfield, the talented speedsters out wide in exile. As the game wore on, the confidence

seemed to drain out of the Men in Black when they were confronted by a desperate, almost frantic, Wallaby side. Then — horror for New Zealand. Carlos Spencer's delayed skip pass was telegraphed, and centre Stirling Mortlock intercepted and sprinted 80m to score between the posts to hand Australia a 7–0 lead. The All Blacks would never recover, eventually losing 10–22. Tana Umaga, unwanted by the coach, consoled Justin Marshall after the final whistle. McCaw walked briskly off the pitch after congratulating the Wallabies. Aaron Mauger seemed almost overcome with emotion as he vanished down the dressing-room tunnel. Another World Cup campaign had come and gone without success.

'We missed a lot of first-up big tackles, and that threw them back over the advantage line,' said McCaw, who had been nominated — alongside Australian flanker Phil Waugh, France's rising star and No. 8 Imanol Harinordoquy, powerful England hooker Steve Thompson, and eventual winner Jonny Wilkinson — for the IRB's Player of the Year award. 'We scrambled really well and made a lot of good tackles. But once they got in behind, that seemed to be where the problem was. They defended well and

It's over. The All Blacks' 2003 World Cup challenge ended with semifinal defeat against the Wallabies in Sydney. The defeat would cost coach John Mitchell his job.

they shut us down everywhere we went. And when they had the pill they really stretched us. [Stephen] Larkham and [George] Gregan, they were running, and put a lot of stress on our defence line, and got momentum and every time they got down our end, they got points.' McCaw said that the All Blacks were expecting the Wallaby halves to run at them after the Australian backline had been written off during the World Cup. 'But the forwards got good ball for them, and the class of those inside backs, Gregan and Larkham, just showed, and we didn't have the answers. Any other day we may have. But they got a roll on and got their tails up. With Larkham and [Elton] Flatley running all different angles, it was hard to know

where to tackle. Hindsight's a great thing, perhaps we could have changed the way we approached a couple of things on defence. But we had a system we thought was going to work, and it has done in the past. Perhaps they had us a wee bit more worked out, but we didn't get to make those tackles that really hurt them.'

McCaw and the rest of the team dusted themselves off and fronted against France four days later in the third–fourth playoff, winning 40–13. A few days later, McCaw was named as New Zealand's Player of the Year. Celebrations, though, were put on hold as McCaw publicly backed Mitchell and Deans to remain in their jobs. Mitchell had won two Tri-Nations and the Bledisloe Cup, had produced stars like Mils Muliaina, Keven Mealamu and Joe Rokocoko, and had the All Blacks playing sublime rugby in the first half of 2003 But his team had peaked too early, and his decision to turn his back on the experience of players like Anton

Oliver, Andrew Mehrtens, Christian Cullen and Taine Randell had come back to haunt him and the rugby nation.

Within a week of the semifinal loss, *Sunday News* was reporting that Graham Henry — the former Auckland, Blues and Wales coach — would be the All Blacks' new coach, supported by assistants Steve Hansen and Wayne Smith. In time, those appointments would be made, and McCaw was many critics' favourite to take charge of the captaincy of the team.

Famed television commentator Keith Quinn, writing in his book *The Journey To Nowhere*, said he would have liked to have seen the then 22-year-old McCaw — 'perhaps our best player' — captain the All Blacks at the World Cup 'despite his relative youth'.

And Doug Golightly, then writing for *Truth*, echoed those thoughts. 'We've gone through a few coaches and genuine leaders haven't exactly been jumping up and saying "follow me", have they?' he wrote. 'Leadership has been a problem for the All Blacks in recent times although the emergence of Richie McCaw as a player of world class who commands respect and who has incredible presence should rectify that. McCaw isn't too young to take on the job vacated by Thorne and if we follow the mantra that states "the game now revolves around the World Cup" then he'll be in premium shape to lead us in 2007. It shouldn't be a big ask for the bloke. As well as having "class" stamped all over him he's also got "genuine leader" tattooed on his forehead. And he's a bloke all of New Zealand will get behind. Of course, the critics will jump up and down saying "he's too young" or "the job will ruin him", which I'd say "bollocks" to. When you've got what McCaw has got then age doesn't come into it. He's either good enough to lead the men in black or he's not. Simple as that. And to be blunt, he's plenty good enough and not giving him the job now would be a massive sidestep. It also wouldn't be the responsible thing to do. Let's hope Graham Henry sees it that way. Make no mistake, McCaw is the man to follow.'

'When you've got what McCaw has got then age doesn't come into it. He's either good enough to lead the men in black or he's not. Simple as that. And to be blunt, he's plenty good enough . . .'

A MAN TO FOLLOW

AT times it is hard to understand why anyone would covet the job of All Blacks captain. Some players are naturally drawn towards leadership — their DNA somehow finely tuned to 'calling the shots' and 'leading from the front'. And it's true that the status afforded to the role equates to life-long recognition and gives the former skipper a better chance to cash in during the many long years after retirement. Of course, the honour of being 'All Blacks captain' is unmatched in New Zealand sport. It is the pinnacle. And because of the lofty expectations and pressures that come with the job, the leader is almost always the first one people turn on when things start to teeter.

Certainly that was the case for Reuben Thorne after the All Blacks were bundled out of the World Cup by Australia in the side's semifinal at the back end of 2003. Thorne had never been able to unite the rugby nation behind him. His tenure at the helm — spanning 23 tests in 2002 and 2003 — was polarizing. It would be too simple to say that South Islanders supported him and North Islanders didn't. Percentage-wise that may very well have been the case, but his disapproval rating had more to do with style than substance. Thorne didn't make his name by delivering stirring speeches to his charges under the goalposts. He was a throwback. The type of captain who lets his actions do the talking.

The trouble was that nothing about Thorne was flashy. There was no question he was an effective blindside flanker. His work rate and tackle counts were often the best on show. But a lot of that yakka was done at the breakdowns — in the shadows of the game's giants. So when the team faltered, the spotlight fell on Thorne. He would be tagged 'Mr Invisible' by his critics. Many New Zealanders wanted to 'see' their captain lead. They wanted their talisman to be blood-splattered and charging, like the great Buck Shelford. They wanted a fist-thumper will a killer instinct, like Sean Fitzpatrick. They wanted anyone except Thorne.

If there was one certainty when Graham Henry agreed to take on the All Blacks coaching job, it was that Thorne would not be handed the captaincy. Henry's captains, when he had been in charge of

Auckland and the Blues before he headed to Wales in 1998, had been Fitzpatrick and Zinzan Brooke. Henry liked his leaders to lead. Justin Marshall and Anton Oliver — both players who had previously captained the All Blacks — were said to have been candidates. They weren't. Henry knew weeks into his job who he wanted for the biggest job in sports.

That it was not Richie McCaw surprised many. But Henry had a plan in play. While it wouldn't emerge until the end of his second year in charge, the Cantabrian was earmarked to take charge from 2006 on. Tana Umaga — the man given the job — had signalled to Henry almost immediately that he would do the job for two years only. Time would prove that that would be long enough for him to establish himself as one of the modern-day greats. And those two seasons would ultimately allow McCaw the breathing space he needed to mature as an athlete and as a man before being handed the controls of the team by the All Blacks selectors.

Umaga was the perfect choice for captain in 2004. The popular Wellington and Hurricanes captain had grown up before the country on Sky's TV screens. In the mid-1990s he was a tearaway wing with a knack of scoring tries on the field and getting into trouble off it. By 2004 he'd grown into being one of the most popular figures in the game, thanks largely to his transition into one of the world's best centres and his wear-his-heart-on-his-sleeve mentality. And because he had been treated so poorly by the previous All Blacks management, his elevation to the top job had the uniting effect that Henry desired. Umaga had wide appeal. He was much-loved, regardless of people's geography, and as the first Polynesian to captain the All Blacks the 'feel-good' factor when he was unveiled as skipper was unmatched.

New All Blacks coach Graham Henry handed the team's captaincy to Wellington and Hurricanes stalwart Tana Umaga.

The positivity continued for Henry when he named his first All Blacks squad for the domestic tests against England, Argentina and the Pacific Islands. Andrew Mehrtens, who had been on the outer since 2002 when the team was under the charge of John Mitchell and Robbie Deans, was recalled. Other new caps included forwards Jono Gibbes, Craig Newby and Mose Tuiali'i; while in the backs, North Harbour and Highlanders fullback/first-five Nick Evans was the bolter, along with fellow newcomers Sam Tuitupou and Rico Gear.

McCaw — who had played a key role in the Crusaders' march to the Super 14 final, where the side lost to the Brumbies — had been rewarded with the vice-captaincy ahead of more experienced forwards like Chris Jack and Kees Meeuws. 'It's quite an honour when I look around the other guys, especially in the forward pack,' McCaw said. 'There's some pretty experienced characters there, who have played a lot of rugby, and I suspect everyone will be expected to show a leadership role in that regard. We've got to make sure we all contribute, because you've got to get everyone's knowledge. It's not just two guys out there, saying what goes. Everyone's got to lead. My philosophy is you just go out and play your best rugby, and that's the way to do it. The vice-captaincy could make me a better player, and that is what you have to make it do. As vice-captain, you are really responsible for a few more things. But you have to make sure it makes you a better player. Because if it makes you the other way, then you are not the right person for the job. I have to believe that I am the right person. And I have to get into it.'

In announcing McCaw as vice-captain, Henry indicated that McCaw would captain the team at some stage in the future. 'It is a step in the right direction for his long-term future,' Henry said. 'It's also very good that he has a lot of experienced players around him in the forward pack who are going to help his development. They will support him.'

McCaw said it was great to hear Henry's comments,

Graham Henry was handed the All Blacks' reins after the 2003 World Cup disaster. Wayne Smith and Steve Hansen were named as his assistants.

but he wasn't going to get carried away with what might happen in the future. 'I've heard Graham Henry said that. To be honest I'm not going to let it worry me or think too much about it. Whatever is in the future I will worry about down the track. This year we just have to focus on one campaign at a time. We have some big tests coming up in the next few weeks. Then we've got the Tri-Nations and the end-of-season tour. It is not up to me what happens in the future. I just have to focus on the now, play well and contribute as much as I can.'

McCaw's leadership would be called on quickly as the All Blacks prepared to open their season with two tests against England, the reigning World Cup champions. Ahead of the opening test in Dunedin, much was made of the 'men-against-boys' vibe to the pending loose-forwards battle. England captain Lawrence Dallaglio and world-class flanker Richard Hill, both 31, shared 138 tests between them at the time. And the third member of their loose trio, blindside flanker Chris Jones, while having only debuted for the team earlier in the year, had a wealth of knowledge that still easily eclipsed that of the All Blacks. McCaw had played against England just once in his 21-test career, and was joined in the back row by debutant Gibbes and No. 8 Xavier Rush, whose sole test had been six years prior.

However, McCaw left the travelling English press corps in no doubt that the New Zealanders would not be overawed, and he insisted that the maturity of the Chiefs captain Gibbes and the Blues skipper Rush meant there was no need for him to take on any mentoring role. 'These guys have led their provincial teams, so there's a lot of knowledge from them that I can draw on,' he said. 'It makes my job a little bit easier; I don't have to do too much different to what I've always done. We've been working well together the last couple of days, so it's quite exciting, the potential is there. It is hellishly important that we start the test season well against England. Playing England is a great chance to make a statement right from the start of the test season. If we can go out and play a couple of good games, it will help us get our confidence back and we'll be going well.'

It was an imposing start to any international season, bringing an altered collection of All Blacks to tangle with the World Cup champions. 'But I like what I see with the personnel here,' McCaw continued. 'They are all tough sorts of characters who like to get stuck in. I am not meaning the physical stuff, because that is what we are picked for, but the guys who have a real attitude. That is what we are going to have to use, every time. We needed to have some who had a win-at-all-costs attitude, whereas in the past we may not have had that, and right across New Zealand rugby we may have lacked that. We have relied on talent, but that does not win games alone. We have got to

Richie McCaw, pictured here videoing his teammates, has much to look forward to under the new All Blacks management, who had him earmarked as a future captain.

use that, but add some steel to it.'

Henry's era got off to the perfect start with the All Blacks embarrassing Sir Clive Woodward's English side. The Dunedin test was won 36–3, and the second test in Auckland finished 36–12. The All Blacks were playing 15-man rugby to near perfection, running in eight tries in the two tests. And the victories were set up by good old-fashioned forward play. The All Blacks eight — newcomers and all — had answered the call. 'It was an outstanding effort for the All Blacks to come together so well in such a short time,' former All Blacks coach Laurie Mains told The Press after the Dunedin test. 'The thrill I got was just seeing eight All Black forwards hooking into it and confronting everything that came to them, and creating a platform for the backs to score some really nice tries. It was very clear the All Blacks were not going to take a backward step. It was good old-fashioned, tough All Black rugby. It was a simple game plan done effectively. That has to be one of the All Blacks' better performances. They were playing the top-ranked team in the world. England were given a lesson. They didn't stay on top of the world for long. You've got to hand it to the whole All Black pack. They played their hearts out. Guys like Carl Hayman, Jono Gibbes and Keith Robinson were outstanding, and Richie McCaw was out of this world.'

After sitting out the second England test with a slight concussion, McCaw was back in the team for the one-off test against Argentina (won 41–7), before being rested for the last of the pre-Tri-Nations outings against a composite Pacific Islands side. That game was won 41–26 and, while it wasn't a great All Blacks performance, it wasn't a step backwards either. So confidence was high ahead of the Tri-Nations. Although the All Blacks had finished 2003 on a low, they were still Tri-Nations champions and hopes were high that Henry would be able to defend that title — and the Bledisloe Cup — won by Mitchell and Deans.

The first test would come at Wellington, against the Wallabies. Revenge for the World Cup semifinal loss was high on the agenda for the All Blacks. '[The Bledisloe] is a very important cup for us,' halfback

The All Blacks pack paved the way for a whitewash of the touring England team in 2004.

Justin Marshall said. 'There's a huge rivalry that has developed between us and Australia. [For them to win it back] they need to win this test. We had blood and guts and sweated it out last year; we don't want to hand it back to them. They held on to it for quite a while and it's a difficult trophy to get back with only two games.'

McCaw would miss the test due to ongoing problems following his concussion. For the third time in six weeks, his No. 7 jersey was passed to Marty Holah; and the Waikato openside was in sublime form as the All Blacks won 16–7. Holah was key to shutting down Wallabies dangerman Stephen Larkham, and he topped both the tackle and hit-up count for the All Blacks in an outstanding all-round game.

McCaw's head problems would continue. Crusaders sports doctor Deb Robinson described McCaw's case as one that does not follow the normal parameters, because he passed the psychometric test after being concussed but was still suffering symptoms. 'We know that the brain will eventually heal itself, but we just don't know the timeframe,' she said. 'The problem with him is that he's not fitting the normal parameters. When he gets to a high level of activity, that's when the symptoms are coming into it.'

Four days after the All Blacks' 23–21 win against the Springboks in Christchurch, McCaw was declared unavailable for the remainder of the Tri-Nations tournament. He withdrew from the squad following discussions with the All Blacks' coaching and medical staff. 'This is the best decision,' he said. 'I am making progress on recovering from the symptoms of the head injury, but there is the added concern of not being match-fit.'

The All Blacks would lose their next two tests — in Sydney (18–23) and Johannesburg (26–40). While not the reason for the losses, there's no doubting that McCaw was missed. *Sunday Star Times* columnist Phil Gifford summed up the views of the nation: 'If you want a reminder of how brilliant a player Richie McCaw is, think about how much we've missed him in

Richie McCaw's head problems would keep him from playing in a number of Tri-Nations games in 2004.

the Tri-Nations games in Sydney and Johannesburg. Marty Holah is a very good player, but I'm one of many who was wrong when I thought there wasn't much between him and McCaw. There is. To be brutally honest, it's gold versus silver.'

With each of the three teams finishing with two wins and two losses, the All Blacks — thanks to their 14-point loss against the Boks — had the worst points differential and were credited with last place. It was a reality check for the rugby nation, and a wake-up call for the coaching staff. Henry, Steve Hansen and Wayne Smith would admit months later that they had over-trained the team while on the road. As a result, many players were burnt out by the time of the Johannesburg test. It was a lesson that would reap rewards in the colossal year that lay ahead.

ON the eve of the biggest year in New Zealand rugby

since the World Cup-winning highs of 1987, Richie McCaw would achieve something he had dreamt about but which he had never allowed himself to really believe would happen.

Before the All Blacks left for their end-of-year tour to Europe for tests against Italy, Wales and France, Graham Henry told the *Sunday News* that McCaw would captain the team at some stage on the tour. 'He is the heir apparent — it's no secret that he will probably be the next All Blacks captain,' Henry said. 'He's going to get some time when Tana is off the field during this series when he will take over the leadership.'

It was another massive vote in confidence in McCaw from Henry. McCaw had returned to action in the Air New Zealand Cup in September — three months after his initial concussion — and captained Canterbury to the championship. Many assumed that Henry would hand the captaincy to McCaw for the final game of the

tour against the Barbarians at Twickenham. Henry, though, had much bigger plans for his openside flanker.

With Tana Umaga at the helm in Rome, the All Blacks cruised to a 59–10 win, the captain and vice-captain combining to score four of the All Blacks' nine tries. And then the announcement came: Richie McCaw would become the All Blacks' 61st captain by leading out the team against Wales at Millennium Stadium. The test was something of a classic, the All Blacks getting home 26–25 thanks largely to Daniel Carter's boot. McCaw won high praise for his leadership under pressure, as well as for his general play.

Graham Mourie, himself a fine opensider in the late 1970s and early 1980s and an acclaimed All Blacks captain, said he rated McCaw as a better openside than the great Auckland, Blues and All Blacks hero of the 1980s and 1990s — Michael Jones. 'Michael obviously has been one of the outstanding forwards

Richie McCaw's first test as All Blacks captain was a close affair, the All Blacks getting past Wales 26–25.

Dan Carter, in his second season in the All Blacks jersey, in action at Cardiff against the Welsh.

in our history, but this was more because of what he could do with ball in hand rather than on the ground,' Mourie says. 'I think Michael was more of a No. 6 or No. 8.'

In making a comparison between these two champions, Mourie and another distinguished former test captain who also excelled in the backrow, Ian Kirkpatrick, emphasized that there have been major changes in the way the openside flank position has evolved, mainly because of law changes. These, they say, have to be taken into account, and so making comparisons between different eras is difficult. Modern openside flankers — such as McCaw, Marty Holah and, just a few years back, Josh Kronfeld — have had to be much more confrontational and aggressive at regaining the ball at the breakdown.

'I was captain for one game. Tana is still there, and I presume the coaches will have him in for this year. Tana is the captain as far as I'm concerned.'

'I think the way tackled ball law is applied now has changed even from the time Kronfeld was playing,' Kirkpatrick told the *Sunday Star Times*'s Lindsay Knight. 'The way things have developed in that part of the game in the past four or five years has been remarkable and not always to the good. Players such as McCaw have to make tackles and then get to their feet to try to force either a turnover or a penalty.'

The former All Blacks coach John Hart, who'd brought Jones into his Auckland side in 1985 when the player was an unknown, had no reservations in comparing McCaw with one of his all-time favourites. 'They're different and with different skills,' he said. 'McCaw's main skill is what he does on the ground, and Michael's was above the ground with the ball in hand. But they are both wonderful players. I think McCaw, like Michael, could play six or eight because he has strength, explosiveness and vision. But he's so good where he is now and with the continuity he provides, why would you do that?'

Another loose forward expert with an awareness of the modern game through coaching, Leicester Rutledge, believed that McCaw was destined to be a legend. 'I guess in time we'll look up at Richie as being up there with Michael Jones,' Rutledge said. 'I don't think we've seen flankers attack the ball on the ground quite like Kronfeld and Richie. They both play very close to the law, it has to be said, but they do know the law. How good is Richie? Well, I think in Marty Holah, Craig Newby and Daniel Braid we've also got three opensides who'd get in most sides in the world. They're just unlucky to be playing at the same time as Richie. He is in a league of his own.'

Former All Blacks captain Stu Wilson was wowed by what he saw from McCaw in Cardiff. 'He's born to lead, he's an outstanding footballer, he's truly world-class, and the captaincy won't be a burden to him,' he said. 'He gave [his teammates] the stink eye when Wales scored that try early in the second half after some poor defensive patterns by the All Blacks. He will lead the team to the 2007 World Cup.'

The All Blacks celebrate one of the team's greatest-ever performances: a 45–6 win against the French in Paris.

Longtime *New Zealand Listener* sports writer Joseph Romanos was another convert. 'McCaw was almost single-handedly responsible for the one-point win over Wales,' he wrote. 'As soon as the selectors deem Tana Umaga's All Black days over, he will step into the position of New Zealand captain as of right. For a man still aged just 23, it might seem too much too soon. But not with McCaw. Given reasonable luck with his health, he will be a fixture in the All Black team for years. By then, he might well have left even Kel Tremain, Ian Kirkpatrick, Michael Jones and the rest in his shadows.'

A week later the All Blacks, with Umaga reinstalled as skipper, produced one of history's greatest performances when they annihilated the French in Paris, 45–6. The New Zealanders were dominant in every phase; McCaw first and daylight second in the battle of the loose forwards. It was a massacre. *Bleu* murder.

McCaw's performance was so good that, even though Umaga had been impressive too, the debate about who should captain the team the following year began to rage again. The *New Zealand Rugby Almanack*, edited by Clive Akers and Geoff Miller, named McCaw in the Team of the Year ahead of Umaga. And Robbie Deans ensured that the debate had some legs when he named McCaw as the Crusaders captain. 'I really enjoyed doing it for Canterbury during the NPC, and

captaining the Crusaders will be quite an honour,' McCaw said. '[Captaining] Canterbury was really easy. I came back halfway, though, and the team had already played a few games, so I didn't have to do a lot at all. It'll be a little different [with the Crusaders], because it'll be from the start of the competition. But a lot of the guys have played a lot of rugby, so it's not a biggie, really.'

McCaw, though, moved quickly to cancel any arguments about the All Blacks job. 'I was captain for one game. Tana is still there, and I presume the coaches will have him in for this year. Tana is the captain as far as I'm concerned. And if Tana carries on playing the way he is, he's definitely going to be there, so it's not going to be an issue. I've just got

As the British and Irish Lions beckoned in 2005, the All Blacks' leadership combo of Tana Umaga and Richie McCaw was very much entrenched.

to go out and play well and prove again that I'm the No. 7 — that's all I am focused on. Then it's up to the coaches to decide who's going to be in their team. But the captaincy thing is out of my hands — it's not something I think about.'

The All Blacks, then, were united and primed for 2005 — and the impending visit of Sir Clive Woodward's Lions.

THERE is something special about a Lions tour. Indeed, arguably the best team to ever tour New Zealand was the Lions side in 1971; a year when men like Gareth Edwards, Barry John and the great Willie John McBride masterminded a series win against the Colin Meads captained All Blacks.

When the best of British and Irish rugby touched down in New Zealand in 2005, it was clear that it was the most anticipated rugby event in the country since the final of the inaugural World Cup in 1987. It helped that the hated England — and their coach from their 2003 triumph, Sir Clive Woodward — were reigning World Cup champions. The incessant gloating from the Northern Hemisphere's media meant that All Blacks' fans were primed to ram their words right down the home unions' collective throats.

It helped, too, that there was history between Woodward and his All Blacks counterpart, Graham Henry. The two had not got along when Henry was in charge of Wales in the late 1990s; something that was ensured when he led his team to a famous win against England at Wembley.

The stage was set for an epic battle, but before the two teams could lock horns the All Blacks had to win their spots in the team in the Super 12. Richie McCaw, for one, was thriving with the Crusaders captaincy. It helped that he had the support of the man he'd replaced, Reuben Thorne. 'Richie is an outstanding young player and a natural leader,' Thorne said the day after McCaw was handed the captaincy. 'I know the coaches have been thinking about Richie for a while, so it wasn't a surprise when he was named. He did a great job during the NPC, and obviously has All Black experience, too. It's not an issue for me. I'm very happy to support him in whatever way I can. There is a lot of leadership right through this Crusaders team

Brian O'Driscoll's — pictured top left — Lions tour would be over within minutes of facing the All Blacks' haka in the first test at Christchurch.

and I just want to contribute in whatever way I can to the team.'

Captaincy seemed to be an easy transition for McCaw. Playing in the No. 7 jersey, he would play the game to the absolute limits of the law. And unlike Thorne, who settled for referee's decisions, McCaw proved early on he would not sit back if he felt that his side was being hard done by. In their season opening 32–21 loss to the Brumbies in Canberra, McCaw questioned South African referee Mark Lawrence on a number of occasions. For much of the game he couldn't understand Lawrence's rulings, and clearly didn't agree with them. '[The captaincy] is something you're learning how to do all the time,' McCaw said. 'You want to do it right, but you don't want to annoy [the referee] as well. As long as you know where they are coming from, I'm happy with that. Perhaps it's something I have to keep working on as well. I felt it was all right on Saturday night. I knew what he was ruling, so I guess that's all you can ask for.'

McCaw acknowledged that it can be a fine line when dealing with the men in charge, and the mood of the game can often dictate a captain's approaches. 'It depends on what that game's like. Sometimes you don't need to at all because things are going well. But when you're on the back foot and you feel you're in his ear the whole time, you can see why they sometimes get a bit short with you. But that's just picking your time. I didn't have an issue with how he was communicating. I knew where he was sitting all the time.'

McCaw impressed, too, when he handled himself with poise and grace after All Blacks teammate Ali Williams stomped on his head in the fourth-round clash against the Blues at Eden Park. Williams was sent off after rucking McCaw in the head as his team crashed to a record 41–19 loss. The Blues lock had been under instructions from All Blacks selectors to improve his discipline, but he lost the plot and was caught rucking McCaw. Television replays seemed to catch Williams aiming at least two more blows towards his international teammate's head. Crusaders coach Robbie Deans blasted the Blues and Williams for their tactics. 'I was disappointed with the response of the Blues when the game got away from them,' Deans said. 'There were three head shots and three lots of stitches in our camp because of that from boots.' On the Williams incident, Deans added: 'The head is sacrosanct. Obviously there was a lot of frustration from them and that's how it manifested itself.' Williams would be banned for six weeks. Only a week earlier, Reds loose forward Daniel Heenan was suspended for three weeks for standing on McCaw's head. But the Crusaders skipper refused to criticize either Heenan or Williams publicly.

Incredibly, some Auckland media blamed McCaw, because, in the Blues game at least, he had been offside more than a dozen times. Wynne Gray, *The New Zealand Herald*'s long-time rugby writer, suggested that the All Blacks' openside flanker might have been getting 'too much latitude from referees because of his world-best reputation'. McCaw's reactions were 'so quick, his timing so sure and athleticism so adept that he tests the eyesight and judgment of all the top whistlers'. He alleged McCaw had 'developed a blink-of-an-eye routine where he tackles an opponent, rides him to the ground and then uses the ball to lever himself back to his feet, then gives the impression his opponent will not release the ball. In fact, McCaw has not allowed his opponent to release the ball at any stage, but the flanker is usually good enough or smart enough to pick his moments.'

McCaw let the outcry wash over him and was adamant 'it's not going to change the things I do. I don't go out there to cheat — it's not cheating until you get penalized. People have got on the bandwagon and got a bit carried away with it, in my opinion. But it doesn't worry me, to be honest.' He also said he was not worried that he might be targeted more by opposition players. 'I'll just carry on doing what I'm doing . . . it's my job to get in there and win the ball.'

Interestingly, McCaw explained that the Crusaders

'It's not going to change the things I do. I
don't go out there to cheat —
it's not cheating until you get penalized.'

take a different approach to opposition spoiling tactics. In McCaw lore, a ruck means 'you've done something wrong before it happens. We go back to the start and figure it out from there. We look more at ourselves to see how we can prevent guys from slowing our ball down . . . rather than what the opposition is doing to stuff things up.' This means taking a long, hard, honest look at individual technique. 'Things like, when you get tackled, if you get the ball away from your body you get a good, effective clean-out. That's the way we deal with it.' McCaw said he was not advocating a tactic referred to in rugby league as an involuntary tackle. 'But sometimes you fight too much and go too far [in the tackle] and you get too tied up and the ball gets slowed down.' The challenge is knowing precisely when to stay on one's feet and when to hit the deck. McCaw said many players' natural inclination was to crab a few extra centimetres of territory. But that could mean the difference between 'five-second [recycled] ball instead of two-second ball. Just by fighting to get that extra few centimetres means [the opposition] get a chance to wrap their hands around the ball and the ball's in the air until you go to ground.' The key, McCaw maintains, is 'to go as hard as you can until you get to a point where you know if you don't hit [the ground] the ball's going to be compromised'. He says there is a fine line between making defenders commit to the tackle and getting quick ball. 'It's something you're always trying to get right.'

After leading the Crusaders to a 33–27 win against the Waratahs a week after the Blues game, McCaw was knocked out and subsequently carted off to hospital in the opening minutes of the match at Loftus Versfeld against the Bulls. He would miss the next four games, returning as a substitute in the win against the Hurricanes a week before the semifinals. 'The big thing is to have your confidence, and I wasn't going to play until I felt I could play 100 per cent confident and could go out there and play normally,' he said the day before his return. 'I didn't want to go out there thinking how I'm going to be. I wanted to go there and

think how I'm going to play.'

McCaw said he took plenty of lessons from the previous year's concussion that he picked up in the opening test against England at Carisbrook. The injury ruled him out of the second test, but he returned to play against Argentina a week later; however, when he realized he was not fully fit, he opted to sit out the Tri-Nations. 'I learned from last year that . . . the big thing was to just do it right and make sure I rested, because that's the only thing that helps you to get things right.'

After the tackle from Bulls prop Richard Bands, McCaw said his next memory was waking up in the changing sheds after being carted under the Loftus Versfeld stands. 'It was a pretty good knock at the time. In that first week I had a pretty sore face where I got hit, but it has been quite different to what I experienced [in 2004]. I just wanted to ease back into it and take it slowly. We have just been monitoring things. It's all been pretty good, but we've just taken a conservative view this time and I feel very confident that I am right to get back in there. Last week I starting itching to want to play and this week, even more.'

McCaw played 35 minutes in the 40–20 win against the Hurricanes, and was slotted into the starting team for the semifinal against the same opposition the following weekend. 'Having him back definitely does give the team a lift,' Chris Jack said. 'When Richie came on last week, everyone was pretty stoked to see him back out there. There had been a bit of concern among the team when he got injured, so it was good to see him back. Johnny [Leo'o]'s played amazingly well, but it's just about the different skills they bring to the game and I think we will really appreciate Richie's ball-winning skills this week.'

Defending with intensity and scrummaging strongly, the Crusaders clamped control on the semifinal in the opening exchanges. McCaw was a relentless menace at the tackle, while halfback Justin Marshall was at the heart of the Crusaders' numerous counter-attacks. The game was effectively sealed on the stroke of halftime when winger Scott Hamilton finished off an 80m team try — the first of a personal hat-trick — that lifted the hosts to an 18–0 lead. They would eventually win 47–7. 'What can you say? That was just a brilliant effort from the Crusaders, something we've come to expect from them,' Hurricanes skipper Tana Umaga offered.

The brilliance continued eight days later when the Waratahs were put to the sword 35–25 as the Crusaders bagged their fifth Super 12 title. McCaw had signalled his team's intent in the opening play of the match by wrapping up Lote Tuqiri, who claimed the kick-off, in a thumping tackle. Phil Gifford, writing in the *Sunday Star Times*, captured McCaw's performance

in the final this way: 'It almost seems redundant to say that Richie McCaw was lethal at the breakdown. The newsflash on McCaw would be if he ever had a game in which he didn't play as if his life depended on it, whether making scything tackles, or attacking in a fury of pumping knees.' McCaw was thrilled to raise the trophy for the first time as skipper. 'It's huge,' he said. 'How great it was for our season to culminate in one big performance. What a way to send off Marshy [Justin Marshall], Maxie [Norm Maxwell] and Hewey [Dave Hewett]. They've put so much into the jersey. Everyone's been awesome and it's great to come out on top.'

With the Super rugby out of the way, the country

The Crusaders celebrate their 2005 Super 12 championship after a 35–25 win against the Waratahs in Christchurch.

could finally focus on what it had been waiting for. Well, almost. Before the Lions series, there was the small matter of a test against Fiji at Albany. New faces in the All Blacks in 2005 included wings Sitiveni Sivivatu and Sosene Anesi, utility back Luke McAlister, halfback Kevin Senio, loose forward Sione Lauaki, lock James Ryan, and front-row forwards Campbell Johnstone and Derren Witcombe. Of all of the newcomers, Sivivatu was the star — something he proved against his countrymen as he ran in four tries in a 91–0 victory.

With that test out of the way, the focus finally fell on the Lions. Before the first test in Christchurch they'd played six tour games: losing to the New Zealand Maori in Hamilton, and beating Bay of Plenty, Taranaki, Wellington, Otago and Southland. Woodward was 'absolutely convinced, more than ever, that we have a team here that can do something special in that first test match. I've got no doubt what we're doing is correct in terms of off the field and how we've organized the trip. It's a tough place to come and it's all about making sure the team is properly prepared for the test matches. I believe we have the personnel within this group and the coaching staff to do something that not many people have achieved in the past.'

In contrast, Laurie Mains — the last All Blacks coach to coach against the Lions (his team winning its series 3–0 in 1993) — couldn't disguise his contempt for Woodward and his cohorts, labelling them the worst Lions squad to hit these shores for 55 years. Mains described the Lions as 'at worst dreadful, at best inept' as he forecast a repeat 3–0 scoreline to the All Blacks. 'The 1966 and 1983 Lions were beaten 4–0 by the All Blacks and Woodward's team doesn't appear to have better players than those teams,' Mains wrote in his *Sunday News* column. 'If the Lions perform at the level they showed in the draw against Argentina in their warm-up game, they are likely to be beaten in New Zealand in several provincial games as well as be hammered in the tests.' Not even the inclusion of

ABOVE: Richie McCaw prepares for the first test against the Lions in Christchurch.

LEFT: Sir Clive Woodward was confident his Lions side would triumph in New Zealand.

England's World Cup hero Jonny Wilkinson had Mains worried. 'Wilkinson is a very fine player. Under normal circumstances he would have been a significant factor. But the Lions are not going to be close enough to the All Blacks for Wilko to have a great deal of effect.'

Before the opening test, Woodward and his veteran No. 7 Neil Back tried some mind games against McCaw. They both talked about the openside flankers being the 'superstars' of New Zealand rugby, as opposed to the goal-kicking first-five-eighths who were more revered in Europe. 'I try not to listen to it too much, to be honest,' McCaw said of the pre-test hype. 'There's always pressure from yourself to do your job. But playing the Lions will be tougher than most times because of the quality players they've got.' Knowing he would be a target of 'cheat' claims at some stage of the tour, McCaw vowed not to change his style but said he'd be mindful of 'what [the Lions] are trying to achieve. You soon see what you want to do, and what you can't. It's something I'm learning all the time. A couple of times in Super 12 you felt like you were being taken out in play. I got quite frustrated at times. But you've just got to find ways [to overcome that], and it means there are opportunities for other people.'

McCaw insists, too, that the key to dominating at the breakdown is teamwork, and implored critics not to focus on any '7 v 7' duel. 'When we play against a No. 7 who's a menace, it's not just [our] No. 7's job to make sure he doesn't do that — it's the whole forward packs. It's not just one-on-one . . . with Rodney [So'oialo], Jerry [Collins] and me, and Sione [Lauaki] and Mose [Tuiali'i], we're working on ways to make sure we can all work together.'

The All Blacks certainly 'worked together' as they steamrolled past the Lions 21–3. They were dominant across the park as Ali Williams and Sivivatu each scored tries and Daniel Carter kicked 11 points. 'The amount of hard work we put in and the pressure we were under — not just from the Lions but from the expectations of our own — paled to the expectations we had on ourselves,' Tana Umaga said. 'We went out there to prove a point. From our last test last year [against France] we wanted to build. We believe we did. But sometimes test rugby can be a bit fickle, and we know we can't back down or take things for granted. This is only one of three, we still have our foot in the door but we haven't won anything yet.' Vice-captain McCaw agreed. 'The guys' reaction at the end of the game was happiness,' he said. 'But we realize that the job has only started. We'll certainly enjoy a win over the Lions, but the job is only a third done and that's the way we've got to look at it. There was a lot of work done, especially from the forwards, and we did a lot of bloody hard work to get the points on the board. I guess the hard work paid off and we've come away with the victory.'

Watching in the stands that night were McCaw's biggest fans — his parents, Don and Margaret, who shared with The Press's Keri Welham the pride they feel for the man they see as 'just our boy'. As the

Richie McCaw, like the rest of the All Blacks, dominated their personal battles against the Lions.

All Blacks thundered around Jade Stadium encircled in a wild southerly squall, Don's mind went back to those Hakataramea Valley days when his only son first played rugby. 'It brings a bit of a lump to my throat,' Margaret said, 'thinking he's out there representing New Zealand.' The McCaws tape every game and watch them again at home. They insist they watch the whole game, not just their son. Don says they do not think of McCaw as a world-best, but they are aware that commentators around the globe do. 'We just see him as Richard.'

At halftime, Don said he was pleased with his son's performance, but there looked as though a bit of father–son coaching might be going down before the next game: 'I don't know about that kick he did up the other side there. I'll have to talk to him . . .'

Controversy raged after the test, when the Lions

claimed that Umaga had deliberately injured Lions captain Brian O'Driscoll, who left the field after just 60 seconds, his shoulder dislocated in a tackle. All Black hooker Keven Mealamu was also implicated by Woodward, who said that the New Zealanders 'intentionally spear-tackled' O'Driscoll. Henry staunchly defended his skipper. 'I can't talk for him. All I will say is he's got a huge amount of respect in our camp. He's a top leader and a top professional and he's got my total backing.'

When Umaga eventually fronted the press, it was clear that the criticism aimed at their skipper had united the All Blacks like never before. Senior All Black hooker Anton Oliver was on Umaga's right flank as Tana prepared to be 'grilled' by the travelling media pack about whether he was a dirty player. 'I'm here because I'm his friend, and he's my captain,' Oliver said. And to Umaga's left stood McCaw, with locks Ali Williams and Chris Jack towering behind. Scattered throughout the room at the NZRU's HQ in Wellington were the rest of the All Blacks. 'The way I play, I play hard. In all my games, I try to play as fair as I can. That's the way I am,' Umaga said. 'I really don't have

ABOVE: Brian O'Driscoll lies injured after being tackled by Tana Umaga. O'Driscoll and the Lions won no fans with their conduct in the week following the first test.

FOLLOWING PAGES: Tana Umaga, Richie McCaw and Tony Woodcock run riot against the Lions.

that much else to say, other than it was an unfortunate incident, and these things happen.'

McCaw paid his own tribute to Umaga by scoring a try in the second test at Wellington — one of five All Black tries in a 48–18 rout. Earlier, McCaw and Aaron Mauger had made stirring 'Let's do it for Tana' speeches before the kick-off. And after the romp, Umaga's Wellington teammate Jerry Collins said: 'It's fine attacking someone in the media, but it's a dangerous game to play and it certainly backfired on them.' And then some . . . 'Although we didn't focus on it a lot, we got together on Friday and said bugger it, if someone is going to have a crack at our leader we'll get round him and do our talking on the pitch

and we did that,' McCaw said. 'He's a superb leader and the guys were there to help him. He's a guy in the team who means heaps. We just thought, let's do our speaking on the park. What happened, we wanted to show we're behind Tana. If anything, it brought us together tighter and made us closer as a unit.'

McCaw said the second test was far more physical than the first, with the Lions players happy to throw punches as they headed towards a series defeat. In one ugly incident, Julian White stamped on Byron Kelleher's elbow and could have broken his arm. 'We expected it [to be physical]. Perhaps last week we expected it, but it didn't happen. But tonight I was sure it was going to happen. As I reflect on this I'll think of it as one of the tough ones, but one where you came out on the right side. We've spent so long building up to this and it's awesome to be involved in this side. We wanted to show we could play any sort of football. When we arrived at the stadium and felt the grass and could see she was dry, you could see from the grins on the boys' faces that they wanted to

have a good game and I hope that showed. There's nothing better than throwing the ball around.'

With the series won, McCaw, who was suffering from a hamstring injury, sat out the third test. The All Blacks were intent on inflicting a third embarrassing loss on Woodward and his Lions. And, remarkably, they did it with ease, despite McCaw *and* Daniel Carter (a late injury victim) being sidelined. With Luke McAlister in the No. 10 jersey on his debut, Umaga led his charges to a comprehensive 38–19 triumph. Woodward was sent packing with his tail well and truly between his legs.

IT would have been easy for Graham Henry's All Blacks to 'clock off' after the Lions series was done and dusted. There had been so much hype, controversy and ultimate glory that the year could already go down as a great one in New Zealand rugby's long, proud history. But the All Blacks of 2005 were a determined bunch. While the players weren't aware of it, captain Tana Umaga knew he would retire at the end of the year. And he was determined to right the wrong that

was his team's last-place finish in the 2004 Tri-Nations before ending his test career, by winning a Grand Slam at the end of the year.

Indeed, propping up the Tri-Nations table the previous season now made it easier for Henry to ensure that his men were determined to maintain their high standards after the departure of the Lions. The All Blacks were certainly battle-hardened as they headed to Cape Town for the opening game against South Africa. They were also confident — perhaps too confident, because their helter-skelter style got kicked into touch by the Boks, who opened with a 22–16 win. The Springboks reigned at the breakdown, where Schalk Burger shaded McCaw's phenomenal work rate. The Cantabrian had a frustrating test, regularly drawing the ire of Australian referee Andrew Cole, who issued a warning after McCaw was penalized at the ruck three times in quick succession during the first half. Henry said the team 'tried to push the boundaries a little too much. We were a bit rusty, we didn't think we would be, but that shows the pressure we were

under from the opposition.' McCaw, too, conceded that the game plan was flawed: 'We pushed a few passes that stuck against the Lions but they didn't [in Cape Town]. We have to be more careful with possession next week.'

'Next week' was a test in Sydney against the Wallabies, and George Smith — their talented openside flanker — made no secret of the fact that the way to beat the All Blacks was to stop McCaw. 'It's been a competitive rivalry between me and Richie, and that will continue,' Smith said. 'Richie has been at the top of the game for a while and the competitiveness is there between me and him. I always want to lift my standards when I'm playing against him. Off the field

Richie McCaw spilt blood for the All Blacks' cause as the team clinched the Lions series with their second-test 48–18 win against the Lions in Wellington. He celebrated with Tana Umaga, before Chris Jack and Ali Williams joined them for an audience with England's Prince William.

we get on, but it's a different story when you're battling to play better than him. New Zealand have a talented back row and we need to contain them.'

As it was, a powerhouse scrum, sensational second-half defence and an electrifying performance from recalled Joe Rokocoko allowed the All Blacks to shatter the sequence of home-team victories in the Tri-Nations and win 30–13, ensuring the Bledisloe Cup remained in New Zealand for at least another year. There had been 11 straight home-team victories before the test, and it seemed that could become a dozen as the All Blacks conceded 13 points in a shocking opening phase. But, in an immensely satisfying performance at a venue where they had crashed to humiliating defeats in 2003 and 2004, they scored 30 unanswered points — thanks to tries from Piri Weepu, Rokocoko and McCaw —to position themselves for Tri-Nations glory.

The All Blacks' forwards coach, Steve Hansen, singled out McCaw for special praise after the match. The Crusaders captain was named man-of-the-match and scored the decisive try, which extended New Zealand's lead to 10 with about 15 minutes left. 'He really stood up this week as he wasn't happy with his performance last week — even though it was pretty good,' said Hansen. 'He has very high standards.' Hansen had become concerned, however, that the smear campaign orchestrated during the Lions series by Clive Woodward to discredit McCaw was still being felt. Woodward and the British and Irish Lions had made a big deal during their tour of how New Zealand loose forwards — McCaw in particular — attacked the breakdown. His aim was to get the referees to focus on McCaw, and Hansen was convinced that referees were targeting his vice-captain. 'He seems to be the one getting penalized all the time, yet everyone keeps telling us he's the best in the world,' Hansen

Joe Rokocoko leaves Wallaby Drew Mitchell in his dust as the All Blacks beat Australia in the 2005 Tri-Nations in Sydney, 30–13.

said. 'The other guys must have improved a lot.' He added there was little that McCaw could do about the unwanted attention: 'You just have to keep playing, and eventually the problem will go away. Clive did a really good job during the Lions tour to make sure everybody thought Richie was a cheat. We know he's not; he's a class player, but obviously he's under the microscope and he's going to cop a few [penalties].'

As a rule, McCaw tests out the ref in the opening minutes and then lives within those boundaries. 'I try to figure out where I am with the ref early on; if I give away a penalty hopefully it's not kickable, but then I know where I am. I am perhaps guilty of getting over-eager at times when things don't go our way; sometimes you try and make up for it by doing things you shouldn't. For me, I was a little disappointed against South Africa, especially giving away those early penalties. I guess that's history now, but looking back I know I've got to pick my time a bit better and make sure those times count. There's always the odd [decision] where you know you're in the wrong, and then there's the odd one where you know you were right, and then there's the 50-50s that could have gone either way. It's bloody hard to ref, there's so many things happening, and I don't know how you could change things to be fair. That's what's so good about rugby: that it is a contest and there's always going to be interpretations that are a bit different. You can go a long way to help yourself a lot of the time by just doing the little things to stop the opposition annoying you, and if you get across the gain line it makes it a lot easier for the ref to rule in your favour, because it means you're going forward and it's more obvious that they're infringing by coming in from the wrong side. It's when you get smacked over behind the advantage line where you end up doing things not quite right. In that regard you can help yourself a lot and make things a lot easier for the ref. But certainly when I look at the TV, sometimes I shake my head and wonder what I'd do there because the ref could go either way.'

After the Sydney test, McCaw said he had his heart in his mouth when he dived over for the try after making a split-second decision to run the ball from a penalty. 'It was all or nothing, because if I didn't score it was probably three points that we'd turned down, so I guess you have to take your opportunity. All the boys stepped up in the second half, and it makes it easy for the loosies if the big boys step up. Finally, we got a bit of luck in the second half. We made a lot of mistakes in the first half and gave away penalties at crucial times and let them in the game. At halftime we spoke about building pressure. We kept putting pressure on and pressure on, and we knew they would eventually crack. There wasn't any panic.'

Many in the media panicked when it was revealed that Carter had badly injured a calf muscle in the game and would miss the rest of the Tri-Nations. But within the camp the team retained their composure. The first-five duties were handed to Leon MacDonald, the All Black fullback who had played first-five in the 1990s for the Chiefs in the Super 12.

The nervous scribes should never have worried; MacDonald guided the team to a 31–27 win. A try from Keven Mealamu with a couple of minutes to go secured the win that McCaw was always confident of getting. 'I never thought we'd lose it — you can never think like that,' McCaw said. 'You've just got to keep believing that you're in with a chance. We were in that position when we were in Cape Town when we were one try away. We felt we had them under pressure, and it was just a matter of patience. Perhaps I was a culprit of not showing patience when I was close to the line, but I guess that's what happens in test matches, you've got to take your chances. I'm pretty relieved we were able to get across.'

McCaw had an epic battle with Schalk Burger, his South African counterpart, in the test that saw the All Blacks debut their new haka 'Kapa o Pango'. 'It's always a tough battle against him. He gets stuck in. It wasn't really a one-on-one battle and you've got to take your chances here and there. He's always a

menace, but in the end we were able to get better ball and that was the key.'

The win in Dunedin set up a virtual Tri-Nations final against the Wallabies at Eden Park — a test where McCaw won rave reviews as he scored one of the All Blacks' four tries in a 34–24 victory. 'Richie McCaw's standing as world rugby's best openside flanker remained intact after last night's Bledisloe Cup test at Eden Park,' the great *Dominion* writer Lindsay Knight wrote. 'McCaw was all energy and revelled especially in the surging drives from rucks and mauls which the All Blacks generated so well in their first half-hour of almost complete dominance. He surged through for the opening try, then was a key man in lineouts not in his usual role as a marauder from the back, but as a jumper at two. He also raced through to take the All Blacks' second spell kickoff and raised a hope that this might be an omen for a final onslaught to take out

Richie McCaw grabs a try in the Auckland win against the Wallabies and (RIGHT) is congratulated by Ali Williams.

Tana Umaga headed off for his final All Blacks tour after leading the All Blacks to a series win against the Lions and victory in the Tri-Nations.

the Tri-Nations title in style.'

Henry was thrilled. After seeing off the Lions, his team had come from last in 2004 to win the 2005 Tri-Nations. 'Considering the quality of the opposition, it was the best rugby we played all year,' he said. 'If we had the bounce of the ball we might have been

up 30 points to 10. We were playing that bloody well. The guys put on the field the game we had practised to play. They implemented the game plan superbly. Although we gave away two soft tries, which was irritating . . . that performance was immensely satisfying as a coach. We're still a maturing team, there's still some way to go and that's good, we've got things to work on. The defence was questionable . . . and we didn't have enough patience on attack. But the results have been outstanding really. If we sat back in January and said we'd win the Bledisloe Cup, the Tri-Nations and beat the Lions three-zip, we'd be pretty happy wouldn't we?'

Umaga, too, was satisfied. 'We're starting to become a really cohesive unit as a side, and I think if you look at the quality sides of years gone by, it's the sides who have stayed together. That's probably something that's come through this year. When you win three trophies, that's got to be something special.'

The next challenge awaiting the team was the Grand Slam attempt at the end of the year. Only Graham Mourie's 1978 side had been able to go to Europe and beat Ireland, Scotland, Wales and England. Umaga was determined he join Mourie as a Grand Slam-winning captain. And Umaga and the team had plenty of motivation. After the All Blacks' series win against the Lions earlier in the year, Lions coach Sir Clive Woodward had taunted the All Blacks despite the New Zealanders scoring 107 points to their 40, and 12 tries to their three. Woodward's parting shot before he left for home was this: the results said nothing about the strength of New Zealand rugby, or rugby in Britain and Ireland. 'I don't think there's any gulf between the Northern Hemisphere and the Southern Hemisphere,' he said. 'I'm looking forward to seeing this New Zealand team take on the four home countries week after week in November when they're all fresh and New Zealand are battered.'

November had come, and the All Blacks were hungry for success. New All Blacks for the tour included back Isaia Toeava and forwards Jason Eaton, Chris Masoe, Angus Macdonald and Neemia Tialata. Henry, intent on building depth for the 2007 World Cup challenge, made it clear early that Umaga would play in only one of two opening tests against Wales and Ireland. He would eventually decide that his captain would miss the Irish test, which meant that McCaw, who would captain the team in Dublin, would start from the All Blacks bench in Cardiff behind Masoe, who had beaten off the challenge of Marty Holah to be McCaw's understudy.

McCaw — who had helped Canterbury into the Air

As the All Blacks attempted to repeat the success of the 1978 side and win the Grand Slam, they took time out to meet the Queen.

New Zealand Cup semifinals before the tour — had no qualms about skipping the Welsh test. 'Obviously you want to play as much as possible, but the coaches have got their plans and they believe you can't play three weeks in a row,' McCaw said. 'If you've got three test matches in a row you can't play to your best, so they've decided the whole squad is used on this tour, and one way of doing that is to mix guys up and have faith in them. We'll see what happens, but if we can get some new guys putting their hands up and getting a taste of international rugby it's got to be good for the team.'

What happened was the All Blacks cruised to a 41–3 win against a poor Welsh outfit. And not much was expected to change a week later when McCaw led the side out against the Irish. Sure enough, they were too big, too fast and far too skilful for Ireland's best as they galloped to a 45–7 triumph. McCaw, after his second game at the helm, seemed destined to take charge of the team sooner rather than later. Certainly the captaincy didn't frighten him. 'Being captain of the

All Blacks in the past was a big thing — along with the coach — and they took the weight of everything,' McCaw said. 'That meant that guys who weren't captain or coach just did their own thing. They only looked after how they played and weren't putting their hand up to contribute to the team. That's changed over the past twelve months. Now we've got a group of guys who have been around for a while and are really contributing to the way the team operates and how we play. That's taken a heap of pressure off the captain. All he's got to do now is oversee everything and go out and play well. That's the way it should be. If there's a time where he needs to say, "I'm the boss and this is what we're doing", that's fine and you accept that. But you've got to give other guys the chance to make decisions and that's only going to make guys stronger. We have a culture where, if you think there's something wrong or you think something needs to be said, you can just say it. No one will bite your head off, because if you're feeling it there's obviously going to be other people thinking the same thing. If we can encourage that, then hopefully we won't have any issues at all.'

One of the most insightful moments about the pressure of captaining the All Blacks was revealed by Reuben Thorne before the semifinal against Australia at the last World Cup. In front of the media, Thorne, who was about to play the biggest game of his life, said that more often than not when All Blacks supporters stop him in the street they didn't say 'good luck, Reuben', but 'don't let us down'. McCaw has had that said to him in the past, too, and says it's a comment that sticks in the mind. 'There's the odd one like that, and, as an All Black, they're the ones you take notice of. A lot of people say good luck, but the ones that make more of an issue are the ones that say stuff like that. The big thing as a rugby player — and especially as an All Black — is that you've got to learn that thinking like that isn't going to help anyone. We don't want to let anyone down. But something we're always learning is to leave that expectation to

the side. The public expectation isn't going to help the expectations already within the team, which are probably even higher than those outside the team. Even if we do our best, some days we will come second. But as long as we perform the way we can, what more can we do? The worst thing is when we come off and think we've played poorly, we could've done better and we've got beaten. That's when it's most disappointing. That's when it feels like we've let people and ourselves down.'

If the All Blacks were going to be beaten on this tour it would be against England at Twickenham; the last game of the tour against Scotland was seen as very much a formality. And the chances of an upset improved when McCaw withdrew late in the week when he was suffering from headaches. Masoe was given the start, and played the game of his life as the All Blacks sneaked home 23–19.

The Grand Slam was alive and well when the All Blacks arrived in Edinburgh. And as kick-off came closer, the enormity of the occasion only grew. Not only was the squad on the verge of joining the 1978 team as Grand Slam winners, they were also about to complete one of the greatest years of All Blacks rugby — a Grand Slam after winning the Bledisloe Cup and Tri-Nations championship, as well as a series win against the British and Irish Lions. And then there was the Tana Factor. The popular skipper had told his teammates that the Scotland test would be his last.

Fittingly, the All Blacks would win 29–10 and Umaga had his perfect ending. There were tears aplenty in the shed after the game as Umaga confirmed his decision to retire. McCaw spoke of his admiration for his captain: 'I think the big thing was that he was honest in what he said. He never said stuff just to please people. When he came to an issue in the team, it didn't matter who it was to, he meant it. What you saw was what you got. There was never anything bubbling below the surface — it always came out and then you can just move on if there was a problem. He's the guy everyone looks to, and he seems to have a pretty cool head and wise things to say. That's going to be a huge loss.'

Two weeks into the new year, Henry hinted that McCaw would take over the captaincy. 'It's obvious, isn't it?' Henry said when quizzed about who would replace Umaga. 'Let's not beat around the bush here. Richie has been the vice-captain and he has captained the All Blacks on a number of occasions for the last couple of years, and he has been groomed for the job. Injuries can happen between now and then, but it's obvious that Richie is the outstanding leading contender to captain the All Blacks this year.'

Laurie Mains was convinced McCaw had to be handed the job. While others were backing the likes of Rodney So'oialo and Anton Oliver, Mains was adamant McCaw was the only choice. He raved about the openside's form as the Crusaders were on the march to their sixth Super rugby title: 'I have had charge of some of the greats of All Blacks rugby in my time. But I'd rate McCaw ahead of the likes of Zinzan Brooke and Jeff Wilson when it comes to being at the top of the pile of players with that telling ability to influence games. And when you add Colin Meads to that mix it's a big call from me, but one I am absolutely prepared to stand by. There is no doubt in my mind McCaw will be named All Blacks skipper this year and rightly so. He has been such a trump card for the Crusaders this season. He is playing at an unbelievably superior level. He just picks up the game when he needs to and he has a huge influence by doing some outstanding things. I don't think I have ever seen a better openside flanker. When we look back at the great players New Zealand has had — the likes of Graham Mourie, Michael Jones and Josh Kronfeld — McCaw stands out above all of them. He is just so strong and is aggressive with it. He is winning lineout ball and he is still doing his job as an openside flanker. If ever there was a complete footballer, McCaw is it. It is unbelievable what McCaw is achieving. He is literally picking up that Crusaders team by the coat tails at times. He did it in Timaru against the Sharks, in

Richie McCaw did his chances of being named All Blacks captain no harm by leading the Crusaders to Super 14 success in 2006.

Brisbane against the Reds and against the Blues and Cats in Christchurch. When the Crusaders are down and out, he has the ability to take charge of the game and lead them to victory. I have never seen a player have as much influence as this guy is having at the moment. He is an outstanding player. And he is doing it as a leader. A lot of captains see their games fall off because of the responsibility and the pressure that comes with the captaincy. But McCaw has lifted his game to a higher level than we have seen in the past. And a lot of it seems to be because he is captain. He cannot bear to see his team not doing well. And when they are not playing well he takes it on his shoulders to lift the whole thing up — and he's doing it.'

McCaw's dominance was even getting to some of his test teammates. When he had the better of the Hurricanes in a Super 14 game in Wellington, Jerry Collins threw the ball at him in frustration and Neemia Tialata throttled him at the bottom of the ruck and punched him in the head. McCaw, ever the diplomat, played down the incidents: 'There's all sorts of things that go on out in the field that perhaps you wouldn't say or do if you weren't on it,' he said. 'But that's the way it is. You walk off it and leave it. That's the great thing about playing guys you know so well — you go hard, as you would against anyone, and then walk off and have a laugh about it. That's what sport is about.'

Two weeks before he named his first squad for the year, All Blacks coach Graham Henry officially named McCaw his captain. 'He will lead from the front,' Henry offered. 'He is probably the most committed guy I have seen play the game.'

One man with a unique insight into McCaw is the All Blacks' former media manager Matt McIlraith. During his tenure with the All Blacks — which ended at the conclusion of the 2003 World Cup — he'd had a front-row seat to the goings-on behind All Blacks' closed doors. The leadership gene, he said, oozed from McCaw.

'The day after the [2003] Rugby World Cup semifinal loss wasn't a lot of fun for anyone associated with the defeated All Blacks camp, but it still contained an incident I won't forget in a hurry. It is a memory that reassures me that the immediate on-field future of All Blacks rugby is in good hands. Back at the team's base camp in Melbourne, I found myself alone in the same room as flanker Richard McCaw. McCaw had given as much as anyone to the previous night's contest, but it hadn't been enough, and the weight of the 22 to 10 defeat by Australia was hanging heavily on his shoulders. His feelings were understandable. Looking around the shattered dressing room in the moments that had followed the final whistle at the Sydney Olympic Stadium the night before, it wasn't hard to imagine what a lot in the room were thinking. "What impact will this defeat have on me?" The anxiety was well founded. Many of that group are no longer involved with the All Blacks, myself included.

'For McCaw, there was one aspect, above just about everything else, that he appeared to find the most troubling: it was that the blame for the defeat would be largely laid at the feet of his good friend, and the team's captain, Reuben Thorne. McCaw did several media interviews in the days during the immediate aftermath of that defeat. In each of them, he spoke of the collective accountability for the defeat, of the great disappointment the squad felt, of how hard everyone had worked, and of how no one, and certainly not the captain, deserved to be singled out for the blame. He also expounded similar views about the coaches, John Mitchell and Robbie Deans. McCaw's staunch defence of his friend and captain, his fierce loyalty to his teammates and coaches, and the integrity he showed in his frankness and preparedness to be accountable for the All Blacks' defeat, encapsulated the qualities that make him such a special person and a fine leader. Watching him then, and since, it's easy to see why he has been pegged as something special. While it's easy to speak such platitudes about teammates and coaches, saying what you think is expected of you, and I've seen so many players do it, but not all of them really mean it. McCaw does. You can tell from the way he delivers his views. With forthright honesty.

'The fact McCaw is such a damn fine player too, is an outstanding tactician, and is as skilful as anyone on the planet at understanding and manipulating the unnatural jungle that is a breakdown in rugby, marks him down as a once-in-a-lifetime talent. It's also the reason why he is going to be such an important figure for New Zealand as the All Blacks prepare for the run-up to the next World Cup.'

McCaw was, quite naturally, thrilled to be given the All Blacks captaincy. 'To be quite honest, just playing for the All Blacks is a dream. When I was young I used to dream about running around with the silver fern on, but the thought [of being captain] as a young fellow never entered my mind, really.'

His parents, too, were overjoyed. 'We hope he can cope with it,' said Margaret. 'We know rugby has such a high profile in New Zealand . . . it worries me a wee bit, but I think [that he will handle the job].' And Don? 'I'm sure he will try his best, give it his best shot whether it's good enough or not. What an honour for him just to play for Canterbury . . . this is unbelievable.'

McCaw's first challenge as All Blacks skipper was to win the pre-Tri-Nations matches against Ireland and Argentina. And he had four new All Blacks to induct: forwards Clarke Dermody, Jerome Kaino and Greg Rawlinson, and wing Scott Hamilton. The All Blacks machine — coming off one of its best years in history — showed no signs of becoming unhinged in this post-Umaga era. The Irish were competitive, as they always are, but didn't have enough firepower to threaten the All Blacks. McCaw's team beat them 34–23 in Hamilton before notching up a 27–17 win in Auckland.

Henry had split his All Blacks squad up before the second Irish test, and sent a number of players to Buenos Aires ahead of a group of 10 from the Auckland test, who followed days later. McCaw was one of the 10 who travelled late to Argentina, but it was never an option to play him. Jerry Collins was handed the captaincy for the one-off game, which would be won 23–19.

The move was designed to keep the game-miles down ahead of an expanded Tri-Nations, in which the teams would play each other three times. And it would be a championship not without its challenges for the new skipper.

Richie McCaw's elevation to the All Blacks captaincy was hailed by many, including the team's former media manager Matt McIlraith, who would wax lyrical about the player's staunch defence of his teammates when things went wrong at the 2003 World Cup.

The first job was to find a successor to Umaga in the All Blacks midfield. In the first three tests of the year, Ma'a Nonu, Casey Laulala and Isaia Toeava all wore the No. 13 jersey. For the Tri-Nations opener the job was given to fullback Mils Muliaina.

The second job was to beat Australia. They did. Comprehensively — winning 32–12. But before the test it was revealed the All Blacks were read the riot act at a special team meeting after accounts surfaced of unacceptable behaviour during the Argentine tour. All Blacks manager Darren Shand confirmed to *Sunday*

'To be quite honest, just playing for the All Blacks is a dream. When I was young I used to dream about running around with the silver fern on, but the thought [of being captain] as a young fellow never entered my mind, really.'

News that the meeting was called in Wellington to state again the high standards of off-field behaviour expected from players — and also to counter fears 'complacency' was creeping into the national rugby team. Asked if player behaviour was discussed, Shand said, 'Yes, those things were talked about. We always run a health check on where we are at. And I guess the management group felt we weren't in great nick on that side of things and that everyone needed to be given a bit of a message about the challenges we have ahead of us and what the landscape will be going forward. We have put the "Better people make better All Blacks" policy out there quite a bit, and that is something that doesn't sit still. It's something we have to keep addressing, because the players live in an environment where there are a lot of pressures and

a lot of temptations and we have to keep addressing that.'

The changing of the guard within the team hadn't been seamless. But McCaw's status was solidified with the win against the Wallabies. A *Sunday News* editorial saw the win as a personal triumph for McCaw. 'The first real acid test for Richie McCaw came last night and he passed with flying colours. Against a pumped-up Wallabies side led by the mercurial George Gregan, the All Blacks needed a top-notch captain to lead them into battle. And that's exactly what they got. Leading from the front, McCaw was into everything, causing chaos at the breakdown which led to Gregan struggling to get quick ball all night. McCaw spoke little to referee Jonathan Kaplan during the game, only giving him a few evil stares when decisions went against the home side. But, by not giving Kaplan an ear bashing like Gregan did, it would have got him in the referee's good books. At one point Kaplan said to Gregan "Mate, go away from me please." With all that McCaw was doing, it was no surprise that he grabbed his fourth try against New Zealand's trans-Tasman rivals. It wasn't the match winner, but it was the one that took the result firmly towards an All Blacks win. The debate is over, McCaw has now found his feet as the All Blacks captain and another piece of the jigsaw puzzle has fallen into place.'

Another convert was the old Australian World Cup winning coach of 1991, Bob Dwyer. 'Earlier this year, after some less than convincing performances against Ireland, there was talk it might take Richie McCaw a fair while to assume the true mantle of captain of this All Blacks team. There's some truth in that. But perhaps, more accurately, the performances against Ireland and by the team against Argentina should be looked at. The "full" All Blacks team didn't assemble until the match last weekend against the Wallabies and it's always easier to captain a stronger team than a weaker one. Once the full team came together, McCaw's captaincy came to the fore and he led the team positively and authoritatively in a quality performance which left the Wallabies with a more-than-clear idea of where they are. Great captaincy is a strange beast. It's a bit like team spirit — you always know when you've got it but you're never absolutely sure how to get there. There are many elements to it, but perhaps the quality that is an absolute necessity is that the captain is an obvious first-choice selection and thereby has the respect of teammates. Courage — especially the courage to remain calm in crisis — is another most desirable quality. Positive and prompt decision-making borne out of this courage goes a long way towards cementing the respect. Last weekend McCaw brought all of these qualities into clear view and the team stayed focused on their direction, despite the early setback of the Lote Tuqiri try which at times in the past might have opened up some cracks in the All Blacks' confidence.'

Next up for the All Blacks were the Springboks. And, again, McCaw's charges responded to the challenge, winning 35–17 — McCaw again on the score sheet.

The team was on a roll — a roll that wouldn't stop until the Tri-Nations championship was secured. A 13–9 win in Brisbane was followed by a clean sweep against the Australians with a 34–27 win at Eden Park, before the title was clinched in Pretoria with an impressive 45–26 victory. That the last game of the series was lost in Rustenburg 20–21 after a moment of madness from Rodney So'oialo didn't seem to matter. McCaw — who would end the year as both the New Zealand Player of the Year and the IRB Player of the Year — had already lifted the Tri-Nations trophy, and a little more than a year out from the World Cup the All Blacks had every reason to be full of confidence.

And that confidence was only strengthened on the end-of-year tour, where wins against England (41–20), France (47–3 and 23–11), and Wales (45¬10) were

Richie McCaw would end 2006 with both the New Zealand and the IRB Player of the Year accolades.

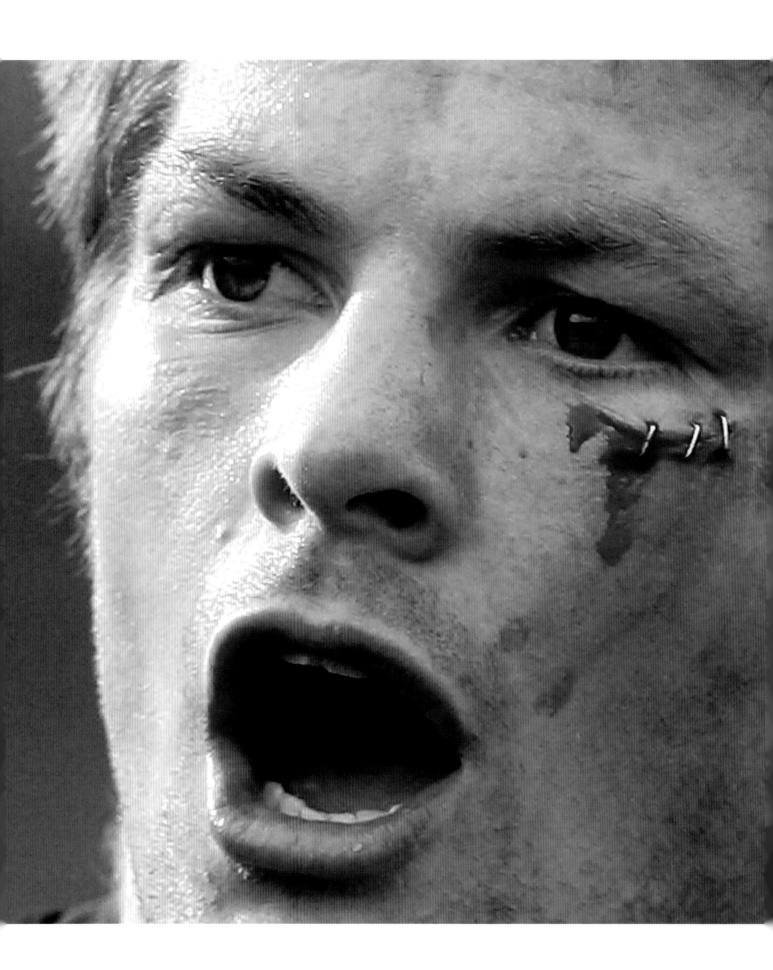

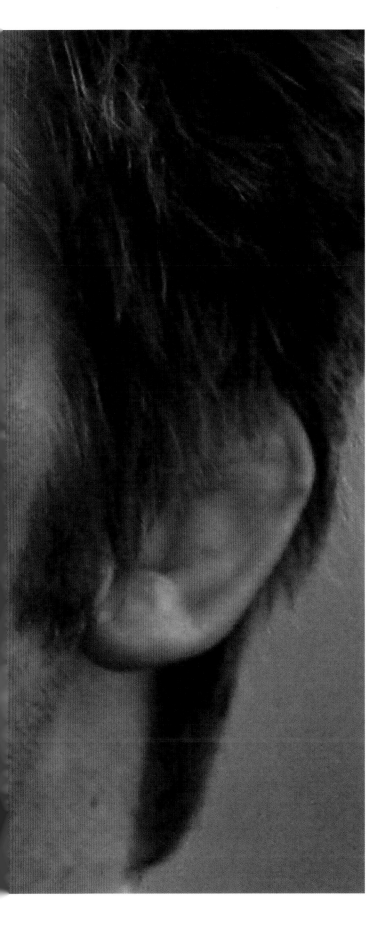

secured. The only thing that stood between World Cup success and the All Blacks at the end of 2006 was Graham Henry's thoughts around reconditioning and rotation — policies that would come to cost New Zealand a massive price in the next World Cup year.

IT wasn't supposed to end like this. Not in a quarterfinal of the biggest rugby show on turf. But the failings that would fall upon the shoulders of Richie McCaw's All Blacks at the 2007 World Cup had been cast in stone by a coach who thought he was doing the right thing when so many around him had been calling for a rethink.

Graham Henry loved rotating his players. In his first four years at the helm of the All Blacks, Henry never selected the same starting–15 in consecutive tests. Never. And in his last 25 test matches of his first four years with the team, he made an incredible 212 positional or personnel changes to his run-on side. That's an average of more than eight changes from test to test. His reasoning was that he wanted to build depth. He wanted at least two world-class players in each position. He fell well short of achieving that, and instead was left with a first-choice team that had never played together on consecutive Saturdays. The principle — to build depth — was sound. The degree to which it was taken was not. The All Blacks' strength over many decades has been built around a solid core. When you look at the great All Blacks teams, they've come at a stage when a team has been together for a number of years and played a lot of rugby together. McCaw's team was never given the chance to reach their full potential at the World Cup, simply because they never played enough tough rugby as a team to be able to cope with the stress and the pressures of knock-out rugby. It was obvious

Richie McCaw — with staples under his eye — captained the All Blacks to 2006 Tri-Nations success, despite a loss to the Springboks at Rustenburg.

that they would be lacking the instinctive knowledge of what their teammates around them were doing, because they hadn't been given the chance to play together week-in-week-out.

Henry's other downfall was his controversial reconditioning programme. Henry, and his assistants Steve Hansen and Wayne Smith, had decided to rest the country's top 22 players by making them sit out the first half of the 2007 Super 14. This meant the players charged with winning the World Cup would start their season playing catch-up. The move was designed to ensure that the players peaked at the World Cup and not in the Tri-Nations. The negative effect of that programme was that it gave the players a sense of security that led to complacency. The All Blacks management spent much of the domestic international season telling us the players couldn't afford to think too far ahead. But the reality was that the day they were named in the conditioning programme, the only thing that would be dominating their thoughts would have been the World Cup. So while it affected them physically, it also affected them psychologically. From the time those 22 players came back into rugby, and particularly when they came to the international season, they never looked anywhere near as sharp or as hungry to play rugby as they had looked in 2005 and 2006. All the conditioning programme did was make some of the players look like body-builders and ensure that when the team as a whole arrived in France we were behind our major competitors in terms of having hard, physical rugby to prepare them for the contests that lay ahead. The only way you get prepared for tough test matches is by playing tough rugby.

All looked to be on track for the World Cup when the All Blacks won the Tri-Nations and Bledisloe Cup with a 26–12 win against the Wallabies at Eden Park in 2007.

FOLLOWING PAGES: Richie McCaw with the spoils of victory.

The tragedy is that the rugby nation was hoodwinked into thinking the team was on the right path. Just as they had in 1999 and 2003, the All Blacks won the Tri-Nations before heading to the World Cup.

McCaw, obviously, was a believer. 'There's a lot of experience built up over the past four years. There's guys here who have played all the way through, and each time you take the field hopefully there's a bit of knowledge that gets banked away to pull out when you really need it. I think I know what to expect a bit more going into this World Cup. I learnt a fair bit last time. But there were things we got wrong and hopefully we'll correct that.'

He admitted he'd dreamt about leading the team to World Cup glory. 'I'd be lying if I said it hadn't crossed my mind once or twice. But we always talk within the team that any game is about performance before the outcome and, hell, that would be a great outcome to be standing there. Whenever I have those thoughts, I think about how I'm going to get there and the hard work that has to go in between now and then.'

Into his second year as skipper, McCaw had matured into his captaincy. 'When you first become captain, you think "Geez, I've got to do this, this and this." But I've worked out that you do what your gut instinct tells you. If you feel you should do or say something and pick your time right, it will become more natural. The other thing I realized is that it's not all about me, either: there are lots of guys that lead this team. It's not just me. You've got to allow others to [to lead], because then it makes it easier. You just go out and play.'

The All Blacks were in a pool with Scotland, Italy, Romania and Portugal. It was a given that they would advance to the quarterfinals — the only question was who their opponents would be. They didn't have to wait long to find out. On the opening day of the tournament Argentina beat the hosts in Paris, which meant it would be the French who would be the All Blacks' eventual opponents in the Cardiff quarterfinal.

Richie McCaw (far right) slumps into the arms of
Ali Williams as the French celebrate their unlikely
World Cup quarterfinal win in Cardiff. The Tri-colours'

LOSING GAMES, WINNING HEARTS

THE cameraman caught the feeling of the rugby nation perfectly. As the referee blew time on the All Blacks' 2007 World Cup quarterfinal, Richie McCaw embraced Ali Williams mid-pitch at Millennium Stadium as French players celebrated. The scene encapsulated yet another New Zealand failure on the sport's global stage — a Cup curse once again enveloping a player regarded as the world's best. Later, as McCaw buried his head at the post-game press conference after the 18–20 loss, he offered the world's media this: 'We can't do anything about it now. It's going to hurt for a long, long time. I'm lost for words . . . We had dreams of what we would do today, but we got beaten by a better team. The pain in the guys' eyes and their body language sums it up. A lot of the guys had been through this experience before, and we knew that the French would be up for the game. We went out there to play our best and we weren't allowed to play our best because of a good French team. I guess the rest is history.'

And although coaches Graham Henry, Wayne Smith and Steve Hansen were a focal point for the inevitable public backlash — along with the New Zealand Rugby Union — McCaw was not absolved from blame. An independent review into the 18–20 loss spread the blame liberally, but it pinpointed McCaw's reluctance to change tack when it became apparent that referee Wayne Barnes would not penalize the French in the second half. A dropped goal was only called for after the All Blacks had moved from a prime position. The blame game was on.

Indeed, it was never really 'off' after Barnes's final whistle. The coaching panel and the NZRU board were public enemy No. 1 for agreeing to and signing off the controversial reconditioning and rotation policies. And given that the quarterfinal exit was New Zealand's worst-ever World Cup performance, the drums were beating for the great Crusaders coach Robbie Deans to be given the All Blacks' reins.

Radio talkback host Murray Deaker — a man who can normally sum up the mood of the country — didn't waste his time laying the blame. Hours after the loss he told his audience Henry should resign at once, McCaw was a poor captain, and the All Blacks'

Ali Williams shows plenty of fire in the pre-test haka against the French in Cardiff.

tactics were feeble — and that was just his opening salvo.

For his part, McCaw — a loyal solider of Deans at the Super 14 level — backed the incumbent coaches to remain in their jobs, just as he had backed Mitchell after the defeat against Australia at the 2003 World Cup. He said the All Blacks had come a long way from 'the first Tri-Nations after [the coaches] took over where we had a bit of a shaky start to where we got to with the depth of players and some of the rugby we were playing. A helluva lot of that comes back to the coaches and the vision of how they were going to get this team running. All three of them have got different strengths they bring to this team and they work really well together. As a captain, you always know there's not going to be anything left out and [the coaches]

will all contribute and have the right say. They've had a vision of how they want this team to go and they've allowed players to lead it, really. That's what these coaches have allowed to happen for the last four years, and that's a great testament to them. A lot of things that have happened in the last three years hasn't suddenly become no good because we've lost one game. A lot of good things have happened. You'd hate to see that start from scratch now. Sure, there may be things you tweak as time goes on. But there's a lot of things that happen now that you'd like to carry on [with] because they work pretty well.'

McCaw said the All Blacks' loss to France was like 'a bad dream' — one he hoped he would 'wake up from'. Although it was his second failure at a World Cup, he felt there were big differences between the

2003 and 2007 exits: 'In 2003 it felt like we didn't fire a shot. [This time] we were firing shots. They may not have been hitting the target all the time, but we were giving it a go right to the end. The guys actually believed we could have got up and we could do something to get out of that game, but it wasn't to be.'

One of the big criticisms of the team's performance — and a key reason for Deaker's assessment of McCaw's leadership — was the decision not to attempt a dropped goal late in the game when it was on offer. Instead of going for goal, the All Blacks stacked up multiple phases in a desperate bid to score a match-winning try. 'It was definitely talked about,'

The three wise men — Steve Hansen, Graham Henry and Wayne Smith — were left embarrassed after the All Blacks' quarterfinal defeat.

McCaw said of the dropped-goal option. 'I guess the guys in those positions have to know when it's on to have a go. Nick [Evans] was there for a while and then Luke [McAlister]. Sometimes when you drop back to do that, the pressure really comes on. The way this team has been it's always backed itself to use the ball effectively. In saying that, you realize you've got to take every opportunity you get and sometimes [a dropped goal] is the only way. From where I was — I can't speak for the guys outside — it didn't feel like we'd got in the right position to comfortably set up for that and the French were aware of that, I'm sure.'

Despite the criticism, McCaw made it clear that he wanted to remain in the skipper's job. 'As time goes on, if I'm still wanted as captain, I'd enjoy doing that, but we'll see what happens when we get back and next year starts up. It'll be someone else's decision. We'll just wait and see.'

While McCaw rallied for his coaches, his teammates lent him support. Reuben Thorne — who'd experienced failure as an All Blacks captain four years earlier — acknowledged skipper McCaw would need support. 'It will be very tough for him. Even more so as captain. But we will stick around him. It's hard. There are no magic words to make it easier.' And prop Greg Somerville, who'd battled back from two Achilles tendon operations and a procedure to correct a torn retina in his eye to get to the World Cup, agreed. 'It's probably pretty tough on [McCaw]. I suppose when he gets home and things get quiet it might be tougher as well. That's where his family comes in and he needs to share some good times with people.'

Certainly McCaw was buoyed by the response he and the team received when they arrived back from Europe in Christchurch. It would take him 40 minutes to make his way through the crowd of well-wishers as he signed autographs and even talked on fans' cellphones to their friends. He said the reception helped ease the pain of the players. 'I'm blown away, I can't believe it,' he said. 'Coming back to this, I don't know what to say . . .'

Ali Williams, the Blues player who would join the Crusaders after the World Cup, made sure he stayed in contact with McCaw and Dan Carter after the tournament. 'The two of them are good now,' he said a couple of weeks after the loss. 'Those guys had a lot of pressure on, more so than a lot of us. People expected not just good things, not just great things, but super-human things — but realistically they're two farm boys, "Dan and Richie", who have great hearts

and basically love what they do. They're human, trust me.' McCaw, a good mate of Williams, took the loss particularly hard. 'I saw him last weekend. We've talked about the loss, but I think it's a male thing to talk about it once, then move on.'

History reminds us that not only did McCaw rightfully hold his job as captain, but the All Blacks coaches survived to live another day. Despite Deans's impressive credentials and an overwhelming mood for change from within rugby, the NZRU gave the incumbent coaches new deals. But such are the workings at rugby's HQ that seven months after the reappointments and the subsequent loss of Deans to the Wallabies, at a time when the New Zealand rugby public was beginning to move on from the Cardiff fall-out, the independent review into the World Cup shambles by Auckland lawyer Mike Heron and former national softball coach Don Tricker was finally released.

The report slated the controversial reconditioning programme, and said that team leadership failed in the doomed campaign's most important moment. NZRU chairman, Jock Hobbs, said that the union and the All Blacks had clearly made mistakes, and they acknowledged them. 'We have previously apologized for letting down our supporters, and I repeat that we are very sorry we failed at Cardiff in the Rugby World Cup, and for the disappointment and frustration this has caused our supporters and our fans.' The report said that time-off for New Zealand's leading rugby players was vital, and other leading nations had off-seasons built into their schedules. Conditioning had succeeded to some degree, with many of the players fitter and faster than ever before, but several struggled

RIGHT: Richie McCaw was left to answer many pointed questions after the calamity in Cardiff.

FOLLOWING PAGES: Some memorable images from New Zealand rugby's blackest World Cup day.

to reintegrate into their Super 14 teams and lacked vital match practice in the cup run-up.

Hobbs said the competition structure was unsustainable and needed to be urgently revamped, but international commitments such as tests and Super 14 meant that there was little room for a rest period to be built into the programmes for top players. A conditioning period was needed, but the way it had been carried out before the World Cup was a mistake. 'The board at that time, when asked to make a decision in respect to it, made a brave decision and one which at that time seemed right. But in hindsight it was clearly wrong, and we accept that.' Henry said ho had undoroctimatod tho impact tho roconditioning programme would have on the players and on the game of rugby in general.

The report also revealed that Henry had sent a message down to the field 10 minutes before the end of the quarterfinal via prop Carl Hayman, who told McCaw to tell the team to try to score a drop goal. The report read: 'In the dying minute of that critical game, the leadership model failed to deliver what was its most important objective — decisions which give the best chance of winning the game. With the benefit of hindsight, the team failed to ensure that the right decisions were taken — players, coaches and management must take responsibility for that.' Despite McCaw's decision to ignore trying to score three crucial points, Henry defended him once the report was made public. 'Richie thought about the decision and made a decision on the park at the time to do what has worked in the past. He made a decision.' Henry said that McCaw had decided it was 'inappropriate to put the acid on [Luke McAlister]', who was on the field in place of the injured Dan Carter.

Laurie Mains — one of the few commentators to predict World Cup failure — was unimpressed with the 'outing' of McCaw in the report. In his *Sunday News* column, he took aim: 'The criticism of the leadership of the All Blacks — and captain Richie McCaw in particular — is hugely disappointing. The

report was edited — meaning the integrity of the document was lost — but for some reason the NZRU was happy to leave in criticisms of McCaw. I find the criticisms really strange, given what an inspirational and great leader Richie is for the Crusaders where clearly he has, through his coach, a Plan B. It is an indictment of the team and the disciplines that he didn't automatically have a Plan B to go to in Cardiff. It was a weak attempt by Graham Henry to say after the report's release that he was standing by his skipper. The damage had already been done. Either the report should never have been released or all of it should have been released. That McCaw can be outed and yet the coaches escape any real evaluation on the job they did doesn't sit well with me. The failure of the

Graham Henry and Richie McCaw, pictured here immediately after the loss in Cardiff, were forced to relive the events of that day when the NZRU released their report into what went wrong.

management to come out and protect their players within the report is indicative of the absolute quest they have to stay in the positions they are in. The NZRU obviously made a lot of mistakes — and serious ones — in the whole preparation in the decisions they made leading up to the World Cup.'

David Moffett — the one-time NZRU boss — was equally dismissive of the report in his column in *The Press*. 'The ill-advised, superfluous and ultimately inadequate and expensive World Cup report has been done to death, but for me the biggest disgrace is the callous disregard for our inspirational captain, Richie McCaw,' wrote Moffett. 'I agree with John Hart when he said on Murray Deaker's show that the coaches should never have made public their instructions to

attempt a drop goal. The union also stands condemned as they had the report for five weeks before releasing it and could have removed that reference from the report as they apparently did with other contentious issues. It resulted in headlines in the UK media about dissatisfaction with the captaincy. Richie did not deserve that and has shown much more dignity and maturity than those who employ him. Yet another example of the union shooting itself in the foot.'

Another high-profile columnist in the Fairfax group — the *Sunday Star Times*'s Phil Gifford — called the report 'clumsy', and said the critical references to McCaw verged on another bout of relentless, self-damaging attacks on an All Blacks captain. 'We went through it with Reuben Thorne, where the verbal assaults became so vindictive it's a miracle he was able to continue. Not many of us would have predicted the same sort of invective being thrown at McCaw, who is patently the best openside flanker in the country.'

The most ill-informed theory floated at the time was that McCaw's position of openside flanker — given the No. 7's work output — disqualifies him from being the captain. Said Gifford: 'Graham Mourie will always be in the grand final of greatest All Blacks captains, and he played all his tests as a flanker. More recently, Sean Fitzpatrick, a hooker, was, quite rightly, revered as a captain. Yet in the front row he had the same view as former Wallabies prop Chris "Buddha" Handy, who once famously said "I saw the whole game through my backside." In passing you might note that, at an equivalent stage of his captaincy, McCaw has twice as good a win-loss ratio as Fitzpatrick did.'

In the World Cup review, where various sections were censored by the NZRU, the criticism of on-field leadership was allowed to stand, including the damaging suggestion that McCaw ignored an instruction to try a dropped goal. Of course, a dropped goal was needed, but by that stage the selection policy of leaving the smartest thinker in the All Black backline, Aaron Mauger, in the stand had come home to roost like a flock of big, fat, flapping vultures.

'The great captains, like Mourie, Fitzpatrick, Buck Shelford, Brian Lochore and Wilson Whineray were clear thinkers, but they also had the benefit of astute tacticians in the backs, who in turn were there as a result of astute selection. On the other hand, McCaw in Cardiff had players picked on promise as much as performance.'

McCaw, obviously, said he was up for the job. And clearly was convinced that being a No. 7 was not a hindrance. 'I guess I am like anyone, no matter what position — you have got to learn as you go,' he said when asked about the damning report. 'I have never said that I have stopped learning. You are learning every time you go out on to the field. I don't see it [playing openside] as being a problem, but I guess everyone has got their opinion.' And on the non-dropped goal? 'You always think about those things. The next time you are in that situation you might do something different. But that is the decision you make on the day and you just have to live with it.'

Hindsight, indeed, is a wonderful thing. With the blame game over and done with, the focus was now very much on how McCaw would deal with the pressures of an All Blacks season played out under the giant shadow cast by the goings-on at Cardiff's Millennium Stadium.

IT was the moment when even his harshest critics finally had to tip their collective hats to the All Blacks captain. A performance that not only was one of the best produced in the famed black jersey, but one that secured his place as of the game's greatest leaders. He could now be mentioned alongside the likes of Graham Mourie, Buck Shelford and Sean Fitzpatrick and no one would dare argue he didn't belong.

Lesser men would have crumbled following the World Cup disaster of 2007. The All Blacks coaches — Graham Henry, Steve Hansen and Wayne Smith — were the main targets of anger from the rugby nation's fans and media, but it was not as though McCaw was left untouched. One of the country's most read and most influential columnists, the *Sunday Star Times's* Richard Boock, penned a piece that left the reader in no doubt that McCaw's days as All Blacks captain must come to an end.

'The World Cup Review Report only reinforced this,' Boock wrote. 'It wasn't the fact that a coach's message had to be sent out to Richie McCaw 10 minutes from the end of the quarterfinal that should worry us. Nor even McCaw's decision to disregard the plea for a drop goal and to keep pushing for a try or a penalty. That was his perogative as captain, surely. No, what was truly astonishing was the revelation that, at the time McCaw and his remaining deputies made their decision, they were apparently unaware that the All Blacks had not received the benefit of a penalty for the entire second half. For 70 minutes they'd been subjected to Wayne Barnes's incompetence and they still hadn't deduced he was the problem. It's barely conceivable. The suggestion seems to be that no one tried to confront the highly impressionable and inexperienced referee; to pressure him about the penalty count or to remind him of his responsibilities, because no one knew they were being shafted. The senior All Blacks didn't know what to do, because they didn't understand what was happening.

'The All Blacks lost because of weak leadership; that much now is clear. Even if McCaw had identified the problem, which he obviously didn't, it's doubtful he possessed the persuasive powers to influence Barnes. Martin Johnson, Lawrence Dallaglio, Sean Fitzpatrick, George Gregan, John Eales, Nick Farr-Jones — they were good captains for different reasons, but they all knew how to engage referees; manipulate them even. The sad truth for McCaw is that he is only a brilliant openside flanker. Nothing more, nothing less. It isn't his fault; the poor blighter probably grew up thinking that would be enough. In hindsight, the decision to appoint him captain was a crucial mistake.'

While not a lone voice in the wilderness, Boock's view wasn't shared by the majority. And McCaw, for one, had already set about ensuring 2008 would be a year of not only rebuilding, but redemption. And when the All Blacks hosted the Wallabies at Eden Park on a cold August evening, McCaw would have the last say on his captaincy credentials.

Before the glories of that night, though, McCaw had begun 'life after Cardiff', rebuilding his confidence and reputation in the Super 14 with the Crusaders. With Robbie Deans in his last season with the franchise before taking on the Wallabies job, there was much to play for. And Deans was backing his skipper publicly when the fallout from Cardiff was at its hottest. 'Everyone knows Richie and his qualities,' Deans said. 'People have criticized him and all I will say about that is "watch this space". Richie will be a lot better for the experience he has been through, and he is not a bloke who will lie down as a result of that experience. He'll grow from it. And [the Crusaders and All Blacks] will benefit from that growth.'

Another keen to support McCaw before the Super 14 kicked off was Henry. With the World Cup Review Report not out until midway through the comp, Henry made it clear before the tournament that McCaw would again be the All Blacks captain in 2008 and beyond. 'We have been delighted with the way he has always captained the side,' Henry said. 'He is a bloody good captain. He is a marvellous player who leads by example and has probably the most successful record of any All Blacks captain of all time if you look at games won and games lost. There is no reason to change. People look at the test match in Cardiff, the quarterfinal, and say, why did we lose that test match? They say the leadership wasn't right, and I would debate that strongly. He captained the All Blacks in that test match like he captains the All Black side in a number of test matches which he has

'Richie will be a lot better for the experience he has been through, and he is not a bloke who will lie down as a result of that experience. He'll grow from it.'

'Everyone wants the magic answer as to why
[the All Blacks lost], but I don't think there is
one basic answer. There was a build-up of
things that just didn't happen that day
and we didn't play that well.
And I still don't know the reasons for that.'

won by doing certain things — which didn't eventuate on that particular day for some reasons which are beyond our control.'

It was a significant decision. Of all of the All Blacks' losing World Cup skippers, only Sean Fitzpatrick had retained the captaincy. And his side's loss to the Springboks in 1995 had been of the heroic variety as they went down in extra time as the team battled food-poisoning. McCaw's side had registered the worst of any All Blacks World Cup finish. But Henry knew the long-term value of McCaw, and backing the Crusaders star for the All Blacks leadership would prove to be a masterstroke.

While the media were reporting Deans's and Henry's musings, McCaw had escaped the spotlight after the World Cup the way he had been doing for years — on an airfield. On the weekend of the World Cup final (between South Africa and England) McCaw was at Rangiora, where he was landing a DC3 at the local air show. As part of his training towards a pilot's rating, McCaw, who is the patron of the Southern DC3 Trust, flew behind the controls of the trust's restored DC3, ZK-AMY. McCaw already had a private pilot's licence with more than 200 hours of flying under his belt. 'I'm pretty happy to get a chance to fly one of these. Not many people with a private pilot's license have this in their logbooks,' he said. 'It was good fun to fly, and it's a lovely old machine. I was a little nervous — it's a lovely old aeroplane and I wouldn't like to do anything bad to it.' McCaw had flown the plane from take-off at Wigram, where it is based, to the landing strip at the Rangiora airport. His mentor and Air New Zealand A320 Airbus captain David Horsburgh said McCaw's flying was impressive: 'It's like he's got 1200 hours already. That was a terrific approach and landing. And he had to do the whole thing himself. It's a very good effort.'

McCaw's real passion away from rugby is gliding, rather than flying. 'Gliding's a real sport,' McCaw said, offering a distinction between the two. 'You've got to get up and look around for places where you can get a lift. The aeroplane is a bit like getting in a car and driving somewhere.' The peaceful moments several hundred metres up are when McCaw can relax. Switching off comes more easily to him than it used to. He believes it is a skill that needs to be learnt. 'The big thing is you've got to have other interests. Then you don't think about the rugby side of things for a while, and all of a sudden you'll think "Hell, I want to get back to rugby." That's the way it should be. If it becomes "Oh, I've got to get back into it", that's not right at all. Flying is something I'm pretty passionate about. I can get away down south where it's nice and quiet. I really enjoy that.'

He also escaped the media's glare by spending time on a farm. His mate Bob Kyle owns a patch of dirt in Springfield near Christchurch. For McCaw, it was a sanctuary from the gloom of Cardiff. 'I didn't do much, just a bit of calf-marking,' he said. 'I rip up there from time to time to shoot a few rabbits, but this was a different [kind of therapy].' McCaw said he needed to think, talk and work at something 'other than rugby. Farming is great for that. There's a couple of other blokes up there I know, and we don't generally talk about rugby.'

The silence wouldn't last. With the Super 14 about to kick off, it meant interviews would have to be done. And talk of Cardiff was never far away. Richard Knowler, *The Press*'s rugby writer, managed to get McCaw to open up about the World Cup and the reaction of the public to the devastating loss. 'I think it was totally the opposite of what you read in the papers,' McCaw said. 'I have not really had a bad word said to me. Obviously the fans are disappointed, too, and they want to know why. That's fair enough. I think they could see we went out there and didn't stop trying. We threw everything into it and that's what people have said to us: "Bad luck, we feel for you." Everyone wants the magic answer as to why [the All Blacks lost], but I don't think there is one basic answer. There was a build-up of things that just didn't happen that day and we didn't play that well. And I still don't know the reasons for that. I think it was a little bit easier with people being quite reasonable about it.'

McCaw, though, did admit that the decision not to attempt a drop goal late in the game gnawed at him. 'It's easy to say now, "Well, shit, penalties weren't going to come and they were defending well", but that's all very well in hindsight. During the game it felt like we were going to get rewarded and it just didn't quite happen. And I would have loved to take a drop goal now — but it just didn't happen. You have just got to learn from that, I suppose.'

With every game put in between Cardiff and the new All Blacks season, McCaw thrived. His form in the Super 14 was back to its best as the Crusaders set about sending off Deans and stalwarts Reuben Thorne, Caleb Ralph and Greg Somerville in style. But despite Deans's four previous championships, his final one held no guarantees of the perfect farewell. The squad for the 2008 edition of Super rugby was without three key All Blacks from the previous season — Rico Gear, Aaron Mauger and Chris Jack.

Jack was replaced by Ali Williams — the troubled Blues lock had headed south to add some steel to the pack. Gear, and in particular Mauger, would prove to be more difficult to cover. Mauger's decision to sign with English club Leicester had created debate as to whether Dan Carter or Stephen Brett would start at No. 12. The other options were to leave Carter at first-five-eighth and use either Tim Bateman or rookie Hamish Gard outside him. Leon MacDonald was another option to play at either first- or second-five-eighth, enabling Deans to shuffle around Carter. Brett could also be tried at fullback. And following the departure of out-and-out specialist Johnny Leo'o, McCaw, too, would be hard to replace if he was injured during the campaign. Rookie George Whitelock was the first-choice back-up to McCaw. Deans had plenty of work to do to mould one last championship side . . .

Typically, though, all of the changes of personnel had little effect on the franchise. The Brumbies were dispatched in week one, before the team headed offshore for the toughest road trip in rugby — back-to-back-to-back games in Pretoria, Cape Town and Perth. All were won comfortably, before the Cheetahs and the Waratahs were put to the sword in Christchurch and the Hurricanes slayed in Wellington. A win against the Lions at home was followed by the team's first loss, in Hamilton against the Chiefs. Deans's men rebounded with wins against the Blues, Sharks and Reds, securing a home semifinal ahead of the last round-robin game against the Highlanders in Christchurch.

The 'Landers surprised many when they stormed to a 26–14 win; a result that had many all of sudden questioning whether the Crusaders had peaked too soon, and had some predicting a semifinal loss to the star-studded Hurricanes side. McCaw put himself, and the team, on the front foot by predicting that much hard work would be put in on the training paddock ahead of the semi. 'Everyone knows it's not about saying things, it's about getting out there and doing it at training. There's no point talking about it all the time. That's what we perhaps found out last week. We all talked the right thing, we just didn't do it.'

The Crusaders responded by trouncing the Hurricanes 33–22 to secure hosting rights to the competition's decider against the Waratahs. Led by a superb two-try display by Leon MacDonald, the Crusaders silenced the doubters who had wondered whether they had it in them. The Hurricanes did score two late tries, to forwards Jeremy Thrush and Neemia Tialata, to close the margin to respectable territory, but this was as one-sided a semi as you will see. The match was dominated by the Crusaders. Their kicking game was superior; their chasing one in another league. Wrote the *Sunday Star Times*'s Phil Gifford: 'The match was dominated by one team, and it didn't come from Wellington. At the front of the charge was Richie McCaw, so dynamic you suspect he may have changed not in the shed, but in a telephone box . . .'

For his part, McCaw was thrilled. 'It's very satisfying, and I suppose the right response after a couple of weeks where we weren't happy with how we played,' he said. 'It was like a different team out there, a whole different intensity, and I am pretty happy with how everybody got stuck in. We got what we were after. We went in at halftime and had spent a lot of energy as well. But they had defended a fair bit so we had to punish them early in the second half. We had a huge amount of territory in their 22 and we had to make it pay in the end and I think it did.'

McCaw, like everyone at the franchise, immediately started playing down the significance of the final being Deans's last game with the team. 'When individuals leave, they don't want it to become bigger than the team. They just want the team to function well, so I think that's going to be the case this week when Robbie goes. He will make sure we don't get carried away. We shouldn't need any extra motivation. That's the way we are going to approach it, and that's the way we have got to. It's just business as usual. I guess the outside influences are talking about it, but we just have to leave that to them and focus on what we do.'

Deans would get his perfect send-off courtesy of a 20–12 win. His side had showed grit and determination to grab a close win against a Waratahs side that matched them in all areas, but in the end the boot of Dan Carter proved the difference. McCaw was the first to pay tribute to the Deans coaching era after the game. 'You can see with the Crusaders every year, no matter the personnel, we're always moulded into believing the same thing, putting the team first. The Crusaders succeed not because of the individuals; the individuals come second, and the Crusaders succeed because of that. That's the thing I've learnt the most being here and playing under Robbie.' McCaw said a vacuum could be created by the departure of Deans and some veteran players, but the coach's legacy would live on. 'Sure, we're going to have big holes left, but I think the value of those guys is that they've taught the next guys to carry on what's happened. There's been a complete change

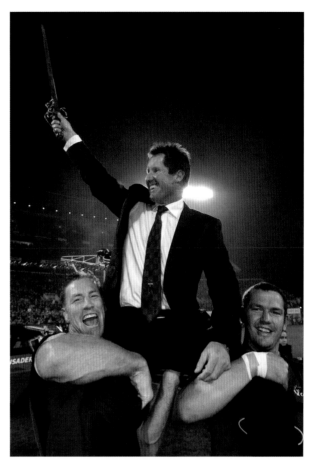

Brad Thorn and Reuben Thorne carry Robbie Deans on their shoulders after the master coach led the Crusaders to another Super 14 title win; this a win against the Waratahs. It was Deans's last game in New Zealand before he headed across the ditch to coach Australia.

in personnel from 1998 when the Crusaders first won to now, but the same ethos and characteristics have been carried through. No matter who you are as a player — whether you're a 50-test All Black or a first-game Crusader — you're all treated the same and you all live by the same values. You go out there to play for your mates and to play for the jersey. That's a huge thing, and we often say "It's better to have a champion team than a team of champions." '

One thing the All Blacks weren't, of course, was champions. But within a week of the Super 14 final, Graham Henry had charge of his team again as they

prepared for life after Cardiff with a one-off test against Ireland and two against England, before contesting the Tri-Nations and the Bledisloe Cup against Deans's Wallabies. Newcomers to the All Blacks squad included Blues wings Anthony Tuitavake and Rudi Wulf, Chiefs first-five-eighths Stephen Donald, Highlanders flanker Adam Thomson, and Blues lock Anthony Boric.

Perhaps more significant was that 14 World Cup All Blacks were missing from the first squad of the season. Jerry Collins, Nick Evans, Carl Hayman, Doug Howlett, Chris Jack, Byron Kelleher, Luke McAlister, Aaron Mauger, Anton Oliver, Keith Robinson and Reuben Thorne had all headed offshore, while Chris Masoe and Isaia Toeava weren't selected, and Joe Rokocoko was injured. Other All Blacks of recent times — Greg Rawlinson, Rico Gear (both overseas) and Jason Eaton and Piri Weepu (not selected) — were also missing. 'There's a lot of new faces, and some guys haven't been here for a while, so it has got a little bit of a different feel,' McCaw conceded. 'The key is that we take the stuff that's worked well in the last few years with the guys that were here. Things will be a little bit different with new personnel, but we have to try and take the good stuff forward, and hopefully be better. It's definitely not starting again. There's no point chucking everything out, because there's a lot of good things that have worked — a lot of good things — it's just a matter of getting the priorities right and getting the things that have [worked]. That's what we've done every year really — you take the things that have worked and throw out the things that haven't.'

McCaw was quick to put a positive spin on any talk of Cardiff, too. 'You've got to get over these things. As soon as we got into the Super 14 pre-season and got a new year started, as rugby players you've just got to get on with it. There's no point dwelling on the past, and now, back in the All Blacks, it's the same thing — you have to look forward. That's been the frustrating thing, that for the whole Super 14 whenever the All Blacks were mentioned it was always looking back. Now we've got a chance to look forward.'

McCaw was in fine form as the Irish were dispatched 21–11 at Wellington, with Sitiveni Sivivatu and Ma'a Nonu touching down for the All Blacks. McCaw's performance and leadership impressed many, including former All Blacks coach Laurie Mains. 'I was fortunate to be the coach of the All Blacks when arguably the country's greatest captain was at his peak,' he wrote in his *Sunday News* column. 'And last night I was thrilled to see Richie McCaw put in a Sean Fitzpatrick-like effort in the All Blacks' first test of the year. In the last three weeks it has been clear that McCaw has decided to play in a "follow me" way. And last night he was so inspirational as the All Blacks got up to beat what was a pretty good Irish side.' And Grant Fox, Mains's former No. 10, was just as woozy in his praise of McCaw in the *Sunday Star Times*. 'As for McCaw, what a performance!' he wrote. 'Right from the moment he led the team out, I could see Richie's hunger. This was an inspired leader's performance, underlining once and for all that we have the best possible captain already at our helm.'

Another impressed was Steve Hansen, the All Blacks forwards coach. 'This was an important game for him, it was an opportunity to say "right, we're moving forward" and give people something positive to talk about rather than all the negativity,' said Hansen, marvelling at how McCaw had transferred his Super 14 playoff form with the Crusaders straight into the test arena. 'He just keeps playing and playing really well. You know when he's really up for it, which is most of the time, I might add.'

The match was McCaw's 23rd as captain, moving him past Taine Randell and level with long-time provincial teammate Reuben Thorne in third on the

RIGHT: Laurie Mains raved about Richie McCaw's leadership in the wet against the Irish in Wellington.

PREVIOUS PAGES: Richie McCaw in action in the 2008 Super 14 final against the Waratahs in Christchurch.

all-time test skippers' list. Sean Fitzpatrick led with 51 tests and Wilson Whineray was second with 30. Hansen believed McCaw would soon be mentioned in the same breath as the latter pair, who had carved a niche for themselves among the great names of the sport. 'I'm sure as time goes by he will become one of our great leaders,' Hansen said. 'He's very much in his infancy as far as captaincy goes. We all know when you first start out as a captain it's not easy. He's done a remarkably good job from the get go, but he's just going to get better and better at it.'

That that growth would be in the black jersey was confirmed ahead of the first test against England in Auckland, when McCaw re-signed with the NZRU through to the end of 2011 and the next World Cup. McCaw's words after announcing his decision would have been music to the NZRU's ears. He spoke of his enjoyment at playing for the All Blacks and Crusaders, and at his excitement over what lies ahead. And he spoke of the money that was on offer from European clubs. '[But] you've got to go for the right reasons, the reasons that stimulate you. If I was just going over there to earn a bit extra, I just wouldn't do that to be honest. I'd have to go because I want to go. At the moment I want to be here playing.' There were factors, he added, at this stage of his career that were not up for the bidding. He also confirmed there was a chance to factor in an extra recovery period into his schedule if required. '[The NZRU] are definitely open to talking about that if required,' he said. 'At the end of the day if you're getting to the point where you need to talk about it you'd be silly to carry on, because you aren't going to last long anyway. I know [NZRU CEO] Steve Tew and the All Blacks coaches are certainly "if you're feeling like that come and talk to us". It's great to know you've got the sort of relationship you can go and do that. I love challenges, and every time you play for the All Blacks it's always a challenge. Super 14 is the same; there's never an easy game. There's the odd time when you don't perform so well, and that annoys you. I get a huge thrill out of going out and

Steve Hansen and Richie McCaw were still going strong in 2008 — seven years after Hansen had given the flanker his first extended shot at NPC glory with Canterbury.

performing, and seeing the team perform well, and when you put the work in during the week and get the reward on Saturday, there's nothing more satisfying than that.'

There was an uncomfortable moment for McCaw ahead of the first England test when Hansen suggested that McCaw was the best openside flanker New Zealand has had. It was hefty praise from the All Blacks forwards coach, as there have been a few decent No. 7s in the history of the All Blacks. Even recent history puts up some reasonable contenders — Josh Kronfeld, Michael Jones and Graham Mourie — but Hansen felt McCaw had it over that trio. 'It is not only his longevity, he is a good link player, a good ground player like Kronfeld was and just a complete athlete,' Hansen said. 'He can do anything. When the

Richie McCaw is flanked by Greg Somerville, Jerome Kaino, John Schwalger and Paul Williams ahead of the test against England at Eden Park.

pressure football has been on, he has been in the front and shows what a great player he is and what a great leader he is. He churns them [good performances] out. He looks after his body and here in the All Blacks, and with the Crusaders, we allow him time to recover early in the week, which can assist him in repeating his performances.' When McCaw was told of Hansen's praise, he was speechless. Eventually he muttered a 'I don't know what to say about that . . .' Finally he admitted it was a nice compliment to receive. 'But you have to keep your feet on the ground. If you start reading too much into that, then you'll come unstuck real quick. There's always good things said and things that perhaps aren't so good. You have to keep looking forward and get ready for a test match on Saturday.

One day, down the track, if they are still saying things like that it will be quite nice, but I don't get too carried away.'

There was nothing uncomfortable, though, about the All Blacks' performance at Eden Park. They dominated the English in every phase as they cruised to a 37–20 win. McCaw had frustrated his opposites so much that England coach Rob Andrew played the role of 'the whinging Pom' perfectly when after the test

he said: 'I'm going to give Richie McCaw an England shirt so when he comes in on our side he's got a white shirt on.' A week later, this time in Christchurch, the result was the same, this time by a scoreline of 44–12. But all was not well in the All Blacks camp, as McCaw limped from the field within the first 30 minutes with a ligament tear in his left ankle.

McCaw wouldn't be sighted in the All Blacks jersey again for six weeks . . . his comeback being at Eden Park against the Wallabies. And, boy, did the All Blacks need him. After the All Blacks had begun their Tri-Nations campaign with a 19–8 win against the Springboks in Wellington, they became the first All Blacks side to lose to the Boks in New Zealand for 10 years, when Victor Matfield's team upset Henry's men 30–28 in Dunedin. Two weeks later, the All Blacks

ABOVE: A week after victory in Auckland, Richie McCaw left the field injured against the Poms in Christchurch.

OPPOSITE: Richie McCaw, Andrew Hore and Dan Carter leave the field after the All Blacks' 37–20 win against England at Eden Park.

were in Sydney for the first battle between Henry and Deans. And it was 'Dingo' Deans who would taste the first blood in the rivalry, with the Wallabies cruising to a 34–19 victory.

McCaw was rushed back into the team for the Auckland test a week later. If the All Blacks were to retain the Bledisloe Cup, this was a must-win test, as game three of the series was in Brisbane and game four on the neutral turf of Hong Kong. McCaw knew he'd have to break through the pain barrier to make an impact. Deans had selected George Smith and Phil Waugh — two recognized No. 7s — for the test. McCaw went into the test on two-and-a-half weeks of running and a combination of cycling, boxing, swimming and grinding in the gym. 'That's never going to make up for the match play. No matter when you start, in the first game it is always tough, so we have got to hope the adrenaline kicks in and you get

stuck in. I'm picking it will hurt, but you just have to get on with it.'

The test would be the first for McCaw against Deans. They had combined for 83 games together at the Crusaders and now they were 'enemies'. 'There is a lot made of what coaches are going to do, but at the end of the day, as a player you are playing against the Wallabies that you have played a lot of times before and have always been tough,' McCaw said. 'You know the players and you know what they are going to bring. That's the way we are looking at it, and I understand they are going to be bringing the same good things they had last week, and, I'm sure, a few things that are a little bit different.'

What was different was the scoreline: McCaw's return coinciding with a 29-point thumping of the Wallabies. The 39–10 win continued an astonishing record for McCaw that had seen him on the winning side in 56 of his 63 tests. Of the 73 All Blacks who have played more than 25 tests, McCaw, on that night, was the most victorious, winning 88.8 per cent of the time.

'His return last night was even more spectacular given how long he has been sidelined,' the *Sunday Star Times* reported. 'Mere mortals might fade in the final quarter of a test when they have been out for six weeks, but McCaw seemed to get better as the test unfolded.' Typically, McCaw played the role of modest hero. 'The game wasn't as quick as it might have been,' he suggested. 'It was a wee bit stop-start, and when you're going forward it makes it easier. But with 10 minutes to go, I didn't have a lot of gas left.'

While there were other heroes, notably prop Tony Woodcock and midfielder Ma'a Nonu, who crossed for two tries each, McCaw's impact had been considerable. The All Blacks were given a hiding at the breakdown in Sydney, but McCaw effectively slowed the Wallabies' ball down in Auckland and he was a key figure on defence. His cool head ensured none of the madcap rugby of the previous two tests was repeated. Henry said McCaw's influence as a

ABOVE: Robbie Deans was reminded of Richie McCaw's brilliant leadership qualities when he returned to right the All Blacks' ship against his men in Auckland.

OPPOSITE: The All Blacks were stunned by Robbie Deans's Wallabies in Sydney in the opening Tri-Nations test in 2008. The All Blacks struggled to contain the Aussies — as seen here with George Smith taking on Dan Carter, Brad Thorn and Jimmy Cowan, with Ryan Cross in support.

player and a leader had been critical to the 44-point turnaround from Sydney, an accolade the man himself was keen to play down. 'Everyone in the XV out there, and the guys that came on, all did their part and made it pretty easy for me. When you come back from not having played for a while, it would be easy to try and do everything. I just wanted to make sure I did my job first and foremost.'

McCaw, who was a frustrated spectator in Sydney, said the reversal hadn't surprised him. 'I was hoping it would happen, because it wasn't a nice feeling last week when we knew we had been out-muscled and had a performance we weren't very happy with at all. I was hoping we'd do what we needed to do, and the pleasing thing was once we got ahead we didn't let them back into the game. The Wallabies are renowned for that. They hang in there and, even though you are on top, the score can be close. That's the great thing — we kept the hammer on them.'

The Sunday columnists waxed lyrical about the country's skipper and his coming of age.

Laurie Mains in the *Sunday News*: 'The return of Richie McCaw made a huge difference. He surprised me with how well he lasted the 80 minutes after a month out. He completely outplayed Phil Waugh and George Smith. I wasn't surprised by the win. The pundits who predicted an Australian win just do not understand the psyche of the All Blacks. Historically, All Blacks teams normally respond when the pressure is on. The losses that have plagued recent New Zealand teams have come when they have been favoured to win. That was the case in Sydney in 2003, Melbourne and Cardiff last year and in Dunedin and Sydney this season. But before the test last night many were picking an Australian win. Indeed, on reflection there was no way the All Blacks would lose the game. Their intensity levels and their passion to restore some mana to the jersey was always going to come through.'

Grant Fox in the *Sunday Star Times*: 'If you ever want evidence of Richie McCaw's standing in test rugby, I offer this match as compelling proof. Richie's

return seemed to infuse the All Blacks with self-belief. A different team turned up last night. They were hurting deeply from last week, and responded in the time-honoured All Blacks fashion. The critical lesson of a convincing victory which we should be celebrating today is you have to turn up both physically and mentally ready to play. Richie personified that last night, and his return kicked off a domino effect that overwhelmed Australia.'

And Phil Gifford in the *Sunday Star Times*: 'Richie McCaw had so many hopes heaped on him, you feared the pressure could be too much, even for someone as talented as he is. He showed his class by not only attacking the breakdowns with his usual ferocity and accuracy but maintaining his composure when the All Blacks were awarded a free kick after 20 minutes. In Sydney there would probably have been a hot-headed tap and run. Last night McCaw called a scrum, the screws were turned on Australia and Tony Woodcock was able to surge to his first try.'

McCaw now had his sights set on the Tri-Nations championship. To manage that feat, his team would need to win in Cape Town and Brisbane. He wasted no time in challenging his charges to aim for the stars. 'We have set a standard now and there are no excuses for not getting back to that level again,' he said. 'I guess it has given us confidence. There is a bit of belief there and we have put the line in the sand now. We have to make sure regardless of what got us to perform [against the Wallabies], we have to make sure we get to that point again. It's a hell of a challenge [in South Africa], but it's something the guys get excited about. The challenge of this pack [in South Africa] — they are a hell of a good tight five and loose forwards — is going to be big for us. You have to get parity up front. The Springboks, they get on top

Dan Carter continued to dominate the No. 10 Tri-Nations battles in 2008, his goal-kicking crucial to the All Blacks' success.

of you and they are a bloody hard thing to stop. They are a little bit different to Australia, but it's the same thing in rugby — if you get parity up front and get some good ball you can use it, so that's clearly what we want to do.'

McCaw was again in sublime form as the All Blacks waltzed to a 19–0 win at Newlands. He put through a grubber kick in the sixth minute to set up Conrad Smith for a try, before Dan Carter took control of the test as the All Blacks held the Boks scoreless in the Republic for the first time. The Springboks took plenty of flak after the game from their press, while McCaw won most of the plaudits as South African newspapers gave their judgment on the goings-on at Cape Town. *The Sunday Independent* said it was a masterly McCaw who ruined what was meant to be a party to celebrate South African fullback Percy Montgomery's 100th test cap. The heights of McCaw's performance matched those of towering Table Mountain, which overlooks the beautiful ground of Newlands, rugby writer Peter Bills said. 'Richie McCaw gave one of the greatest displays in world rugby to shatter the new world champions in their own backyard. South Africa finished a fumbling, disorganised, broken outfit, laid to waste by the genius of McCaw on the floor and his brilliant reading of the game allied to coruscating tackling.'

Also in the *Independent*, fellow rugby writer Gavin Rich said a visitor from Mars would have been unable to tell which team was rebuilding and which team had won the World Cup and had a massive advantage in experience. 'Certainly on this evidence, it is the new-

LEFT: Ma'a Nonu, Richie McCaw and Greg Somerville in full voice ahead of their 2008 test against the Springboks in Cape Town.

FOLLOWING PAGES: Richie McCaw and Rodney So'oialo lift the Tri-Nations and Bledisloe Cups, respectively.

look All Black team, who won through their mastery at the breakdown that are the team on the up. After this three-try to nil drubbing, the Springboks will know that they will have to pull off a miracle if they are to place the Tri-Nations trophy alongside the World Cup they won just 10 months ago. If the All Blacks were the masters, the master-in-chief was McCaw.'

A rib injury meant that McCaw would miss the 101–14 win against Samoa in New Plymouth, a game that was organized to cover the three-week break between the tests in Cape Town and Brisbane. Deans, too, used the time well as he plotted ways to limit McCaw's breakdown prowess. Wallabies tight-head prop Al Baxter admitted Deans had not held back on disclosing areas of McCaw's game that could be exploited as the Australians looked to keep the Bledisloe Cup series alive and win the Tri-Nations at Suncorp Stadium.

'I think he gives good insights into what is effective against him, because obviously Richie's played under him for probably close to a hundred games,' Baxter said. 'Robbie would know what has been effective against Richie and what hasn't been — that's probably the insights we get. But Richie is a great player in his own right, and despite all those insights you still have to actually do it on the field. [McCaw] thrives on getting in there and being a presence at the breakdown. If you take that space away from him, he can't physically get in there to cause the damage he's done. A lot of it this weekend is making sure we take that space and get in that space first.'

The plan almost worked, the Wallabies leading 17–7 just after halftime. But a storming finish would see McCaw's men triumph 28–24 as they secured both the Tri-Nations and the Bledisloe Cup for another year. The All Blacks rattled up three tries in 17 minutes to win their fourth consecutive Tri-Nations title, but they weren't safe as, with two minutes left, a late try by Wallaby Ryan Cross narrowed the gap. Desperate defending followed before the final whistle saw McCaw and his jubilant team embrace as they

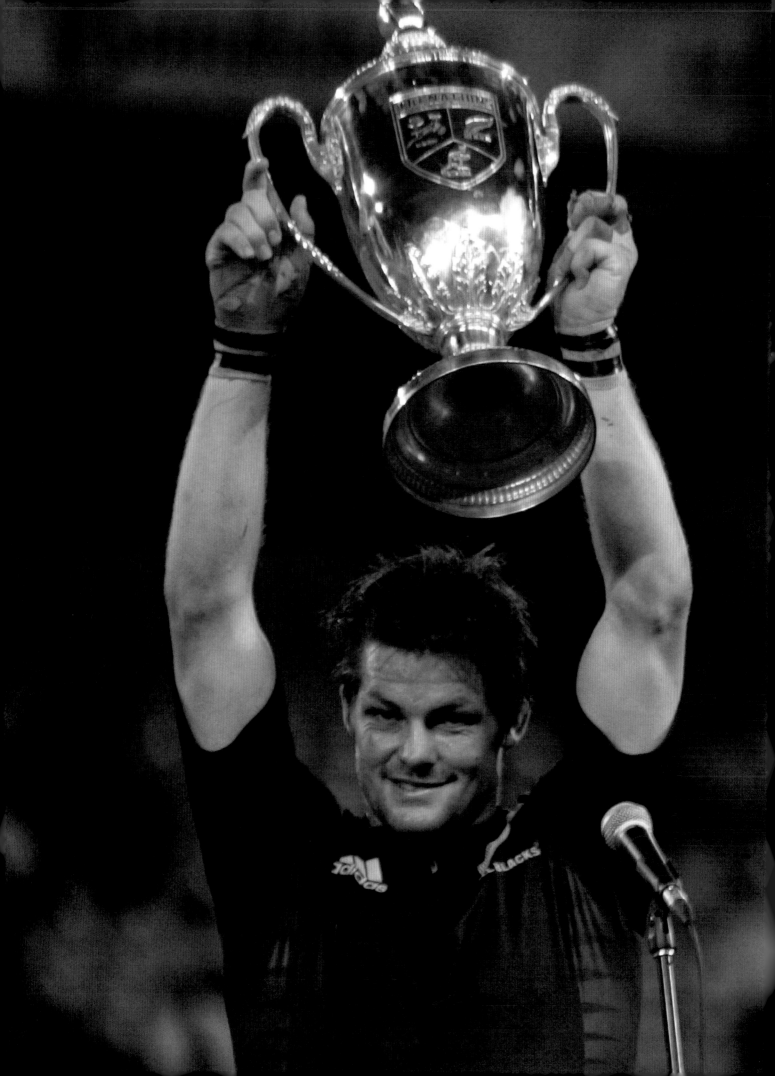

celebrated another famous win. 'We struggled to get into the game,' McCaw said. 'We were up 7–3 but hadn't played a lot of rugby. They scored before and after halftime, and that can be quite critical. We had to make sure we didn't panic and believe[d] in what we're doing. The guys who've been around a while led that, and we got back into the game.'

Henry, whose All Blacks coaching career neared its lowest ebb after the 19–34 defeat in Sydney, gave the win a five-star rating amid his five-year tenure. 'I'm just delighted with what the guys have done. It's a very sweet feeling. This is the fourth Tri-Nations in a row, and Bledisloe Cup, and it's probably the sweetest victory that we've had. There's a large number of new guys who haven't played in this competition before. Half of them hadn't played before, so we were team-building as well as trying to be competitive and we came through, so that's a good feeling.'

The turning point in the All Blacks season was clearly the return of McCaw to the side after his ankle injury. He and his teammates had ensured that the feel-good factor of All Blacks rugby was back.

THERE is something special about All Blacks' end-of-year tours. The television pictures that stream in from grounds like Twickenham, Murrayfield and Lansdowne Road remind many of their youth and times of family get-togethers on hot summer mornings watching men like Graham Mourie, Stu Wilson and Hika Reid do battle against the giants of the Northern Hemisphere.

And while those 'battles' aren't as great as they used to be — given the All Blacks' dominance over the Home Unions — there is still a certain magic that is garnered when New Zealand's best attempt a Grand Slam. Mourie's team in 1978 and Tana Umaga's in 2005 both achieved the rarity of consecutive wins against Ireland, Wales, Scotland and England, and at the end of 2008 it was Richie McCaw's turn to try to match them.

Having been an integral part of the 2005 side, McCaw knew of the demands that would come onto his team. But rather than fear them, he embraced them. And he wasn't the first McCaw to do that on foreign soil.

Fresh from helping Canterbury to the Air New Zealand Cup title, on this tour McCaw was 27 — the same age his exhausted grandfather Jim McCaw had been when he returned to an uncertain future in New Zealand after a notable shift at the coalface on behalf of the 'old country' with the 486 'New Zealand' squadron based at RAF Tangmere and Marston. His flying duties were many and taxing — he flew over 300 operational sorties, mainly in Tempests — but in the summer of 1944 he was exclusively employed taking out the murderous V1 and V2 missiles that the Nazis randomly launched at London, looking to kill or maim as many citizens as possible. *Hiwa hau Maka* — Beware the Wild Winds — was the squadron's motto.

The Hawker Tempest MK5 — armed only with four Hispano 20mm cannon — was brilliantly manoeuvrable at low speed, the fastest piston plane engine in the RAF, and McCaw and his colleagues defended the realm with typical Kiwi tenacity. Officially, he was credited with 19 kills but he also managed to shepherd — wingtip — a number out to sea when he had run out of ammunition. Thousands, probably tens of thousands, of Londoners owe their lives to Richie McCaw's grandfather and his colleagues. On one evening alone in July 1944 he destroyed four V2s heading towards the suburbs, finishing his patrol by scraping into Biggin Hill well past midnight with his fuel tanks showing empty.

A couple of days after that epic, he was awarded the Distinguished Flying Cross. The citation read: 'Flight Lieutenant McCaw has completed a large number of sorties, involving many successful attacks on the enemy's railway communications, mechanical transports, and other targets on the ground. He has also participated in several attacks on shipping, during which time 73 vessels have been destroyed. He is a most efficient flight commander, whose ability and keenness have been reflected in the fine fighting qualities of his flight.'

'The "old fella" was a great man, and we were very close before he died in 1996,' McCaw recalls. 'I stayed up at the family farm in Kurow regularly in the holidays — he used to run a gliding school there — and sometimes we would disappear and go fishing and he would tell me all the old war stories. I dare say he embellished some yarns, and others he must have told me a hundred times, but the really scary ones he made light of or just didn't mention at all. You had to talk to his mates in the bar to find out the truth about those.

'There's a famous piece of footage — it's in all the World War documentaries — which is taken from the gun turret of a Tempest and the pilot has possibly misjudged his approach. Anyway he was very close when he finally managed to loose off his cannon effectively and blow it up, and the pilot had to fly through the explosion and all the shrapnel and debris. It's pretty terrifying. Carnage. That pilot was the old fella. He came out of the other side.'

Others didn't. It was a game of Russian roulette. Ten of Jim McCaw's immediate colleagues and friends in 486 were killed that summer by V2 explosions as they attacked the bombs with suicidal bravery. In total they destroyed 223 missiles headed to England's shores.

'The whole family was — is — very proud of him,' says McCaw. 'Like so many young Kiwis, he did what he felt was the right thing when [the Second] World War was declared and joined up to fight for the old country. He was proud of his Scottish roots — his grandfather was born in the Borders — and safely sitting out hostilities from 10,000 miles distance wasn't an option. That's how it was in those days. Nearly 12,000 of those young Kiwis didn't come back.

'Flying is in the family. Or it is now. The old fella was the pioneer, although I'm never quite sure why he opted for the RNZAF when he joined up. A hidden dream perhaps or possibly youthful bravado? My dad and uncles all fly, and me as well. I learnt to fly exactly where the old fella learnt.

'I lead a very lucky and privileged life and want for nothing, but if I could be granted one wish it would be to tog up and fly for real in a Tempest. Just to get a feel of what it was like and experience in a very small way what he went through. I'm told they were incredible, very fast and untouchable in a dive, but I'm not even sure there is one left in the air, although there are a couple in museums.

'He wasn't a rugby man really, but he was a great support in my career until he died. The moment he saw I loved the game he was on the touchline in all weathers with the family. I wish he had still been alive for my All Blacks debut. That would have meant a lot.

'Of course, his experience — and that of every serviceman — puts sport in perspective. When I travel these days to Britain or Europe with the All Blacks I give my heart and soul for the New Zealand cause — I know of no other way to play rugby and am so proud captaining the All Blacks — but ultimately, in the big scheme of things it's still not a matter of life and death. That thought helps if things go wrong.'

For this Tour of Duty, McCaw would have seven new All Blacks to help induct: Ben Franks, Jamie Mackintosh, Scott Waldrom, Kieran Read, Liam Messam, Hosea Gear and Cory Jane. And with a cash-strapped NZRU desperate for a big payday, the Grand Slam would have to wait an extra week as the All Blacks and Wallabies went head-to-head in Hong Kong. The test would net the NZRU $4 million, but it did nothing for the purists. With the Bledisloe Cup already secured, there was nothing on the game, which the All Blacks won 19–14 — McCaw scoring one of the All Blacks' two tries.

McCaw would be on the bench for the first of the

FOLLOWING PAGES: Richie McCaw in full flight against Ireland's Paul O'Connell (left) and Jamie Heaslip (right) at Croke Park in Dublin on the end-of-year 2008 tour.

Grand Slam games against Scotland. Keven Mealamu was given the captaincy, as the All Blacks fielded a back row of Liam Messam, Adam Thomson and Kieran Read. It was a gamble of sorts, but the Scots were woeful and the All Blacks predictably cruised to a 32–6 win.

The All Blacks were back to full strength for the second test of the tour — in Dublin against the Irish. And McCaw knew that Ireland's star trio — captain Brian O'Driscoll, first-five Ronan O'Gara, and lock Paul O'Connell — spelt trouble. 'When you have fellows like Brian O'Driscoll and Ronan O'Gara, who have played a lot of tests, they are smart players. If you give them good ball to operate with, they have the ability to use it. Maybe the Scottish haven't got a player of world class like O'Driscoll. A guy like that can make a difference. O'Connell in the second row is another one of those characters. With those guys scattered through a team, they lift the players around them. If you give them a bit of an opportunity, you are in trouble. [And] the Irish definitely have the skill-set. But there is very little between top international teams. You look across them all in terms of the skills they have, and it's pretty hard to say there's too much difference. It comes down to how you turn up and the passion that is involved with it. For the first 40 minutes [against Australia in Hong Kong] we were out-passioned. There was nothing to do with skill — Australia just had a little bit more about them than us, a little bit more energy at the breakdown, they were hitting it a little bit harder. Because they got on top, we came out after halftime and actually managed to turn that around. This week will be no different. If we let the Irish get on top, anything can happen. That's the way we are approaching the game — we have to start well, with that intensity.'

Richie McCaw plays the bagpipes on Calton Hill in Edinburgh during the build-up to the test against Scotland at Murrayfield.

The first half was a torrid affair with the scores locked at 3–3 after 37 minutes, before McCaw broke the deadlock on the stroke of halftime with a timely penalty try. As it was, the Irish wouldn't score again. Brad Thorne and Ma'a Nonu each touched down in the second half, the All Blacks taking out the game 22–3.

Next up was Wales in Cardiff. That game will forever be remembered for the stand-off between the teams after the New Zealanders performed their pre-match haka. The Welsh refused to back down, the teams left standing and eyeballing each other. It was spirited stuff from the Welsh, but spirit doesn't win test matches. Their lack of self-belief was evident early in the second half when the All Blacks upped the physicality. The Welsh — the reigning Six Nations champions — wilted, and the All Blacks went on to post a comfortable 29–9 win. The Grand Slam was alive and kicking, with England at Twickenham awaiting the men in black.

While the 2008 squad were not yet playing with the panache of their 2005 Grand Slam-winning predecessors, there had been no shortage of character and composure on display. McCaw's All Blacks had fought back from consecutive Tri-Nations losses in Dunedin and Sydney to win their last eight tests, often from positions of adversity. The Wallabies were in control in Brisbane and Hong Kong before the All Blacks finished strongly; Ireland and Wales also watched combative first-half performances neutralized after halftime.

The team's leadership group's ability to hold their nerve had not escaped McCaw. 'I think that's a positive from the year,' he said. 'And with the experiences you go through, you'd hope it would improve. We've had to come from behind and, although that's not the plan, I guess the good thing is when it doesn't happen the senior players have kept believing in what we're doing. It would be easy to start making more mistakes when you get under pressure: that's what's been pleasing this year — we've absorbed the pressure and taken our chances.'

Naturally McCaw had been the guiding force of the leadership group, and the team steadily rebuilt after the standard post-World Cup player exodus. 'The experiences you go through definitely make you stronger. A year down the track I've learnt to back my gut instinct, what you believe in and stuff like that. Hopefully I'm better than I was back then. The other thing that's key is to keep performing yourself. If I look back on the year, I've been reasonably happy I've done that. That's the first thing you've got to do as a captain.' But McCaw was quick to credit the presence of the senior All Blacks who'd also stuck around for a difficult season. 'They've gone through another year and played another 15-odd tests as well. A lot of them have 50 to 60 tests now, that has to make the team stronger.'

The English game was always going to be a formality. The team was in another rebuilding phase and, although the great Martin Johnson had taken over, they had suffered humiliating losses to Australia and South Africa ahead of the All Blacks test. And Johnson's luck didn't change against McCaw's charges. The final score was 32–6; Mils Muliaina (two) and Ma'a Nonu getting the tries, with Dan Carter kicking 17 points. 'The tour was long and it was tough, especially with an [Air New Zealand Cup] semifinal and a final just before we came away,' McCaw said. 'It's easy to think it's only five games, but it's all the rest that goes with playing for the All Blacks. It's different to playing five Super 14 games. In past end-of-year tours, by the last game we've dropped off the pace, but I was pleased with the way everyone made sure we were "up".'

The Grand Slam had been claimed for only the third time — and it had been done in grand style. The All Blacks didn't concede a try in their four Grand Slam tests. The last test try they'd let slip was to Wallaby wing Drew Mitchell in the 25th minute at Hong Kong Stadium. So at the end of the Twickenham test they'd gone 375 minutes without conceding a test try. 'That's an outstanding stat, and it's credit to our defence and

Richie McCaw becomes the first All Blacks or England captain to raise the Sir Edmund Hillary Shield after the All Blacks' Twickenham success.

the way we didn't infringe and backed our "D" and systems,' Muliaina said. The flipside of the defence was that the All Blacks scored three tries in the final 22 minutes at Twickenham, giving them 14 tries from the five tests on tour. It was heady stuff.

The All Blacks, under McCaw's leadership, had been so successful that even McCaw's harshest critics were forced to backtrack. Richard Boock — who had earlier called for McCaw to be replaced as captain in his *Sunday Star Times* column — showed plenty of class when he publically apologized to McCaw as the Slam was being won. '[I] was no better than anyone else in April, when [I] responded to the World Cup Review Report by questioning McCaw's future as captain and calling for him to be stripped of his leadership responsibilities. [But] whatever the perceived failing, one should always consider the potential for growth and self-improvement. Adversity (be it World Cup disappointment or trying to ride your first bike) shouldn't be the end, but the beginning. McCaw is merely the latest example of this. Since the nightmare of Cardiff, the All Blacks captain has simply emerged from his shell as a leader. Whether he took umbrage at the earlier reports or simply resolved to take some of those criticisms on board is neither here nor there. The upshot is that he has assumed a much more visible command of his team, and is more noticeably at the nerve-centre of operations. His ability as a player might still be progressing in degrees, but his leadership has flourished in leaps and bounds.

'The most impressive aspect? That would have to be McCaw's decision to engage himself more with the referees and to use his considerable experience, understanding of the game, and (not least) his outrageous talent, to gain an advantage. One of the criticisms earlier this year was that he didn't

Richie McCaw played for the Barbarians in a losing effort against the Wallabies at Wembley, after the All Blacks' Grand Slam winning tour in 2008.

carry the same persuasive powers as, for example, Martin Johnson, Lawrence Dallaglio, Sean Fitzpatrick, George Gregan, John Eales or Nick Farr-Jones. It's time to rethink our stance on that. With these extra tools in his kit, and his near superhuman exploits in the black shirt showing no sign of diminishing, it's at least clear from this viewpoint that McCaw could easily be championed as the finest rugby player in the world.'

McCaw's progress in 2008 was probably best summed up by Boock's colleague at the *Sunday Star Times*, Phil Gifford. Formerly based in Christchurch, Gifford had been an eyewitness to McCaw's rise through the Canterbury and Crusaders ranks years before. If anyone was in the perfect position to assess his progress, it was Gifford.

'The most inspiring aspect of the All Blacks' revival this year has been the leadership of McCaw, who is currently running at a 90 per cent winning rate in tests,' Gifford wrote. 'He now not only puts subtle pressures on referees, but also has players in his own side on the verge of whiplash as they swivel to get orders from him when play breaks down. He stays calm when the going gets niggly. You can go to the bank on the fact that McCaw's answer to dirt will be to aim for a bunch of tries, not a bunch of fives. How dominant has he been as a captain? When he missed three tests with injury in the middle of the Tri-Nations, the All Blacks lost two of them.

'He also plays a vital role as a highly acceptable face for All Blacks rugby. Sarcasm, often near the surface in the coaching staff, is not part of his persona. You don't need to worry about public relations when McCaw is captain. There's no real divide between the man and the public image, so being decent and polite to people isn't something he needs to work on with a consultant. In an increasingly competitive battle for the hearts and minds of New Zealand sports fans, it's a stroke of rare good fortune for rugby that it has someone virtually the epitome of a good, keen man in charge.

'The foundation, of course, is what McCaw does as a player. I've been lucky enough to watch Waka Nathan, Graham Mourie, Michael Jones and Josh Kronfeld at the height of their powers. After Nathan I never dreamed I would see as good an openside flanker. Mourie's genius rested in almost preternatural anticipation and application, but he wasn't blessed with the physical strength and explosiveness of Nathan. Then Michael Jones arrived. As strong in testing, All Blacks trainer Jim Blair would report, as a test prop, with the vertical leap of a test lock, almost as much speed as a test wing, and as skilled as a first-five-eighths. Kronfeld was a superb player, on the ground and running with the ball, but if only one player could wear the No. 7 jersey in a game your child's life depended on, only a toss of a coin could separate Jones and McCaw. That's how good he is.'

Typically, McCaw deflected the accolades coming his way by talking up the contribution of his coach. Many, of course, wanted Henry replaced a year earlier. But McCaw was adamant that Henry and his two assistants, Wayne Smith and Steve Hansen, have their contracts extended through to the end of the 2011 World Cup immediately. 'What they have done this year, under the scrutiny, and to bounce back from the disappointments of last year, just speaks volumes for them. They work outstandingly together, so I can't see why they shouldn't stay on.'

McCaw said the coaches had the players' support. 'There's a belief in what we're doing. It would be easy to believe we got it all wrong over one game last year, but we've done a lot of good things over the last four years. We had to make sure we kept those things. It would be easy to say we got it all wrong, but we didn't.'

There was a nice twist of irony late in the year when the draw for the New Zealand-hosted 2011 World Cup was held in London. The All Blacks were drawn with Tonga, the top Americas group qualifier and the top Asian group qualifier . . . and France. The All Blacks had been knocked out of two of the last three tournaments by France, losing the 1999 semifinal in London and then that horror quarterfinal in Cardiff. But the All Blacks can also point to a victory over France in their only World Cup win when they beat them in the inaugural 1987 final at Eden Park. 'There will be a fair bit of talk between now and then about playing France,' McCaw said after the draw was made.

He's right. The All Blacks would lose to the French at the beginning of the 2009 domestic test season

In 2009, injury ruined much of the Super 14 for Richie McCaw — but he was still able to lead his charges all the way to a semifinal against the Bulls.

FOLLOWING PAGES: For the second year running Richie McCaw returned to the All Blacks set up after time out injured to inspire a victory against Australia at Eden Park. McCaw was in sublime form as he scored a try in the 22–16 win — a performance that Laurie Mains suggested proved the skipper is the best forward New Zealand rugby has ever produced.

with McCaw out injured after a torrid Super 14 where he led his young charges all the way to the semifinals. Thank goodness, then, that the All Blacks captain has matured into a leader of men who doesn't just talk the talk, but one who walks the walk as well. He has made it easy for the rugby nation to fall in, in every sense, behind Richard Hugh McCaw as he sets his sights on World Cup glory. Just like Flight Lieutenant McCaw before him, not fronting for the biggest test of his life is not an option. McCaw will lead the All Blacks into battle in 2011, his credentials unquestioned. The All Blacks supporters, finally, united.

STATISTICS

ALL BLACKS GAMES

(c) = captain

2001

17 Nov	v **Ireland** at Dublin 40–29	
24 Nov	v **Scotland** at Edinburgh 37–6	
1 Dec	v **Argentina** at Buenos Aires 24–20	

2002

15 Jun	v **Ireland** at Dunedin 15–6
22 Jun	v **Ireland** at Auckland 40–8
13 Jul	v **Australia** at Christchurch 12–6
20 Jul	v **South Africa** at Wellington 41–20
3 Aug	v **Australia** at Sydney 14–16
10 Aug	v **South Africa** at Durban 30–23

2003

14 Jun	v **England** at Wellington 13–15
28 Jun	v **France** at Christchurch 31–23
19 Jul	v **South Africa** at Pretoria 52–16
26 Jul	v **Australia** at Sydney 50–21
16 Aug	v **Australia** at Auckland 21–17
11 Oct	v **Italy** at Melbourne 70–7
17 Oct	v **Canada** at Melbourne 68–6
	(used as a reserve)
24 Oct	v **Tonga** at Brisbane 91–7
	(used as a reserve)
2 Nov	v **Wales** at Sydney 53–37
8 Nov	v **South Africa** at Melbourne 29–9
15 Nov	v **Australia** at Sydney 10–22
20 Nov	v **France** at Sydney 40–13

2004

12 Jun	v **England** at Dunedin 36–3
26 Jun	v **Argentina** at Hamilton 41–7
13 Nov	v **Italy** at Rome 59–10
20 Nov	v **Wales** at Cardiff 26–25 (captain)
27 Nov	v **France** at Paris 45–6

2005

10 Jun	v **Fiji at Albany** 91–0
25 Jun	v **British and Irish Lions** at Christchurch 21–3
2 Jul	v **British and Irish Lions** at Wellington 48–18
6 Aug	v **South Africa** at Cape Town 16–22
13 Aug	v **Australia** at Sydney 30–13
27 Aug	v **South Africa** at Dunedin 31–27
3 Sep	v **Australia** at Auckland 34–24
5 Nov	v **Wales** at Cardiff 41–3
	(used as a reserve)
12 Nov	v **Ireland** at Dublin 45–7 (c)
26 Nov	v **Scotland** at Edinburgh 29–10

2006

10 Jun	v **Ireland** at Hamilton 34–23 (c)
17 Jun	v **Ireland** at Auckland 27–17 (c)
8 Jul	v **Australia** at Christchurch 32–12 (c)
22 Jul	v **South Africa** at Wellington 35–17 (c)
29 Jul	v **Australia** at Brisbane 13–9 (c)
19 Aug	v **Australia** at Auckland 34–27 (c)
26 Aug	v **South Africa** at Pretoria 45–26 (c)
2 Sep	v **South Africa** at Rustenberg 20–21 (c)
5 Nov	v **England** at London 41–20 (c)
11 Nov	v **France** at Lyon 47–3 (c)
18 Nov	v **France** at Paris 23–11 (c)
25 Nov	v **Wales** at Cardiff 45–10 (c)

2007

2 Jun	v **France** at Auckland 42–11 (c)
9 Jun	v **France** at Wellington 61–10 (c)
16 Jun	v **Canada** at Hamilton 64–13 (c)
	(used as a reserve)
23 Jun	v **South Africa** at Durban 26–21 (c)
30 Jun	v **Australia** at Melbourne 15–20 (c)
14 Jul	v **South Africa** at Christchurch 33–6 (c)
21 Jul	v **Australia** at Auckland 26–12 (c)
8 Sep	v **Italy** at Marseille 76–14 (c)

23 Sep	v **Scotland** at Edinburgh 40–0 (c)
29 Sep	v **Romania** at Toulouse 85–8 (used as a reserve)
6 Oct	v **France** at Cardiff 18–20 (c)

2008

7 Jun	v **Ireland** at Wellington 21–11 (c)
14 Jun	v **England** at Auckland 37–20 (c)
21 Jun	v **England** at Christchurch 44–12 (c)
2 Aug	v **Australia** at Auckland 39–10 (c)
16 Aug	v **South Africa** at Cape Town 19–0 (c)
13 Sep	v **Australia** at Brisbane 28–24 (c)
1 Nov	v **Australia** at Hong Kong 19–14 (c)
8 Nov	v **Scotland** at Edinburgh 32–6 (used as a reserve)
15 Nov	v **Ireland** at Dublin 22–3 (c)
22 Nov	v **Wales** at Cardiff 29–9 (c)
29 Nov	v **England** at London 32–6 (c)

2009

| 18 Jul | v **Australia** at Auckland 22–16 (c) |

POINTS SCORED FOR THE ALL BLACKS

	Tries	Cons	Pens	DGs	Points
v Australia, 3 Aug 2002	1	–	–	–	5
v Italy, 13 Nov 2004	2	–	–	–	10
v British and Irish Lions, 2 Jul 2005	1	–	–	–	5
v Australia, 13 Aug 2005	1	–	–	–	5
v Australia, 3 Sep 2005	1	–	–	–	5
v Australia, 8 Jul 2006	1	–	–	–	5
v South Africa, 22 Jul 2006	1	–	–	–	5
v France, 11 Nov 2006	1	–	–	–	5
v South Africa, 23 Jun 2007	1	–	–	–	5
v Italy, 8 Sep 2007	2	–	–	–	10
v Scotland, 23 Sep 2007	1	–	–	–	5
v Australia, 1 Nov 2008	1	–	–	–	5
v Australia, 18 Jul 2009	1	–	–	–	5
TOTALS	**15**	**–**	**–**	**–**	**75**

Stats accurate up until 24 July 2009

TEST RECORD BY NATION

	Played	Won	Drawn	Lost	Tries	Cons	Pens	DGs	Points
Argentina	2	2	–	–	–	–	–	–	–
Australia	16	13	–	3	6	–	–	–	30
British and Irish Lions	2	2	–	–	1	–	–	–	5
Canada	2	2	–	–	–	–	–	–	–
England	6	5	–	1	–	–	–	–	–
Fiji	1	1	–	–	–	–	–	–	–
France	8	7	–	1	1	–	–	–	5
Ireland	8	8	–	–	–	–	–	–	–
Italy	3	3	–	–	4	–	–	–	20
Romania	1	1	–	–	–	–	–	–	–
Scotland	4	4	–	–	1	–	–	–	5
South Africa	12	10	–	2	2	–	–	–	10
Tonga	1	1	–	–	–	–	–	–	–
Wales	5	5	–	–	–	–	–	–	–
TOTALS	**71**	**64**	**–**	**7**	**15**	**–**	**–**	**–**	**75**

Stats accurate up until 24 July 2009

FIRST-CLASS RECORD
CRUSADERS

	Played	Tries	Cons	Pens	DGs	Points
2001	2	–	–	–	–	–
2002	12	2	–	–	–	10
2003	12	7	–	–	–	35
2004	13	5	–	–	–	25
2005	9	1	–	–	–	5
2006	13	2	–	–	–	10
2007	8	2	–	–	–	10
2008	14	2	–	–	–	10
2009	8	1	–	–	–	5
TOTALS	**91**	**22**	**–**	**–**	**–**	**110**

CANTERBURY

	Played	Tries	Cons	Pens	DGs	Points
2000	1	–	–	–	–	–
2001	9	4	–	–	–	20
2002	8	1	–	–	–	5
2003	–	–	–	–	–	–
2004	6	2	–	–	–	10
2005	3	–	–	–	–	–
2006	1	–	–	–	–	–
2007	–	–	–	–	–	–
2008	3	–	–	–	–	–
TOTALS	**31**	**7**	**–**	**–**	**–**	**35**

ABOUT THE AUTHOR

This is John Matheson's 15th book. In 1999 he collaborated with Eric Rush on the bestseller *Gold Rush,* and in 2000 he penned the critically acclaimed *Black Days* — a series of interviews with rugby superstars recounting their experiences of playing against the All Blacks. In 2002 there was another number-one bestseller, *Rushie* — the second book with Rush — and a biography on league star Stacey Jones.

That was followed by **Life on the Run**, the number-one bestselling biography on All Blacks great Christian Cullen — the third biggest-selling rugby book in New Zealand history.

In 2004 he completed the Rush trilogy when he wrote *Adrenalin Rush*, and a year later he wrote *Tana Umaga: A Tribute to a Rugby Legend*, a celebration of the 2005 Grand Slam-winning captain's career.

In 2007 he had two more books released: the critically acclaimed *All Whites '82*, the inside story of New Zealand soccer's greatest World Cup campaign, which he penned with Sam Malcolmson; and *Andrew Mehrtens: A Tribute to a Rugby Genius*. In 2008 his biography of Warriors and Kiwis star Monty Betham was published, along with his biographies of Wallabies coach Robbie Deans, All Blacks great Wayne Shelford and motorsport legend Scott Dixon.

Early in 2009 his book on former Silver Fern, cancer survivor Marg Foster, was released to rave reviews.

Throughout his 23 years in journalism, Matheson has worked in Auckland, Christchurch, London and San Diego, and has covered such diverse sporting events as the Rugby World Cup, Grand Slam tennis, World Cup soccer, the NBA and the America's Cup.

In New Zealand, he has worked for the *Auckland Star* and *Sunday Star*, contributed to *The New Zealand Herald* and *The Dominion*, and is still the longest-serving editor of NZ Rugby World. He is a former editor of the Qantas Award-winning *Sunday News* sports section.

Matheson — a six-time recipient at the Qantas Media Awards and a nine-time finalist at the National Sports Journalism Awards — directed the Sky TV rugby show Offside. He lists completing the Ironman, playing for and coaching Auckland basketball teams, climbing Japan's Mt Fuji, and being offered a trial by Harry Redknapp at Bournemouth as three of his proudest achievements.

He wishes to thank HarperCollins's Bill Honeybone, Lorain Day and Kate Stone for their support throughout this project.

Matheson dedicates his part in this book to his daughter, Ava-Dawn May Matheson, who was born on 3 February 2006: 'My daytime, my night-time — you are my world.'

Harper*Sports*
An imprint of HarperCollins*Publishers*

First published 2009
HarperCollins*Publishers (New Zealand) Limited*
P.O. Box 1, Shortland Street, Auckland 1140

National Library of New Zealand Cataloguing-in-Publication Data

Matheson, John, 1968-:
Richie McCaw : a tribute to a modern-day rugby great / John Matheson.
ISBN: 978 1 86950 806 7
1. McCaw, Richie, 1980- 2. Rugby Union football players—New Zealand
—Biography. I. Title.
796.333092—dc 22

ISBN: 978 1 86950 806 7

Cover and internal design by Dexter Fry

Printed in China by Bookbuilders Ltd, Hong Kong

PHOTO CREDITS

Air Force Museum of New Zealand: 10

The Press: 14, 17

TRANZ/Corbis: Cover, 4–5, 13, 81, 90, 124

TRANZ/Reuters: 6–7, 8–9, 12, 16,18, 20, 21, 22–23, 25, 27, 28–29, 30, 31, 32, 33, 35, 37, 39, 41, 43, 44, 45, 46, 47, 48, 51, 52, 53, 54, 55, 56, 57, 58–59, 60, 61, 63–64, 65, 67, 69, 70, 71, 72–73, 74, 74, 75, 76, 78, 79, 80, 83, 86–87, 89, 92, 94–95, 96, 98, 99, 101, 102 (top), 102 (bottom), 103, 105, 107, 108, 111, 112, 115, 116, 117, 118, 119, 120, 121, 123, 126–127, 130, 134, 137, 138–139

TRANZ/Rex: 26, 68, 85, 132

TRANZ/Zuma: 2, 135,136